D1621472

Praise for *Elaine Young*

Every teacher should read this book. It demonstrates what is possible in education: students working together to learn from their interests. I am a blade of grass *describes a classroom experience that works and examines a process not usually taught in education courses. Elaine Young has found a way to tap into the natural curiosity of children, fostering their individuality while promoting cooperation within the group.*

Laura Holmes, educator
Mill Valley, California

As one of Elaine Young's colleagues, I can say that she challenged each of us to examine our own motives and expectations as educators. We did not, at times, agree with Elaine's view of "how it should be done," but her profound child-centered thinking caused many of us to focus clearly on personal, pedagogical convictions, readjust our thoughts where necessary and follow more faithfully our educational commitments. Thank you, Elaine, for your impact.

Dr. Diane Garner, teacher
Harrison, New York

In three and one-half decades, I have been associated with many teachers. Among them, Elaine Young stood out and encouraged me to believe that certain people can capture the art *of teaching. . . .We who are dedicated to education must be dedicated to those rare teachers who have the courage to do whatever must be done to make learning possible.*

Dr. Joseph Carbone
Harrison Central School District
Harrison, New York

I have known Elaine Young since she was an early childhood teacher in the laboratory school at SUNY-New Paltz. She was then and continued to be throughout her teaching career a most creative and industrious educator. . . .Now after more than 30 years of experience, Elaine has written a book about her unusual and challenging instructional mode. I highly recommend it as must reading for all creative educators.

Dr. Frederick Bunt, Dean
School of Education, 1966–1983
Pace University, New York

As a trustee and former president of the Board of Education, I know Elaine Young to be an inspiring, dedicated, thought-provoking and loving educator. The children who have been exposed to her teaching methods have come away with a deep appreciation of learning within a stimulating classroom experience. Elaine typifies the true meaning of the word "teacher." I am proud of her achievements and involvement in our school district.

Pat G. Gizzo, J.D., Trustee
Board of Education
Harrison Central School District
Harrison, New York

The concept of hearing how children can learn is one of the secrets of true education. Thank God for books that encourage listening!

Sara Miller
White Plains Public Library
New York

I am a
blade of grass

A Breakthrough in
Learning and Self-Esteem

Elaine Young

with Robert D. Frelow, Ph.D.
Edited by Anne S. Kipp
with a foreword by Barbara Dana

Jalmar Press
Rolling Hills Estates, CA

I AM A BLADE OF GRASS

Copyright © 1989 by Elaine Young

Jalmar Press
45 Hitching Post Drive, Bldg. 2
Rolling Hills Estates, CA 90274-4297

Library of Congress Catalog Card Number: 88-83564
ISBN: 0-915190-54-0
Printing: 10 9 8 7 6 5 4 3 2 1

To Abe, Jeff, Ben and the memory of Sharon

Acknowledgements

So many people have encouraged and inspired me. I wish I could mention all those who have believed in me and made this book possible.

My family, Abe, Jeff and Ben; Anne, Max and Hy, gave me unfailing love and understanding.

Sara Miller, my librarian friend, had the original inspiration.

Bob Frelow was the essential catalyst. He listened to me, responded and heard this book begin.

Anne Kipp put the words in order, always keeping the "Elaine" and always putting our love for the children first.

Lauralee Alben; Tony and Matthew Arkin; Dr. Fred Bunt; Superintendent Joe Carbone; Barbara Dana; Jim Faris; Soichi and Misao Furuta; Rena Hersh; Laura Holmes and the Education Network; Sheila Jackman, Ph.D.; Dorothy Leech; Edna Lipman; Suzanne Mikesell; Judge Sondra Miller; Barbara Solonche; Rachel West; Brad Winch, who took a stand on publishing for self-esteem; and so many others who supported and helped in a hundred ways.

Foreword

A few months ago, my son returned from the opening session of a college course. "Nothing drives me up the wall like a bad teacher," he said. "It makes me crazy. Why can't school be like an exciting adventure?"

The professor had apparently started off by telling his students what a tough course it was going to be, how it wasn't going to be any fun and how they were probably not going to like it. He had added that anyone who thought the course was going to be too much should leave.

My son was livid. "What a way to start," he said, "turning everybody off! This teacher has no passion for his subject. He seems bored and disappointed with life, and he is about to pass those feelings on to all his students. He has no self-esteem, he is filled with disappointment and he seems determined to see that none of us makes out any better than he did. He is single-handedly about to ruin the experience of film-making for twenty people."

My son had obviously thought about this all the way home from college. "I had some great teachers in high school," he continued. "Even my Spanish teacher, who was a little vague sometimes, loved Spanish, and welcomed the chance to pass her enjoyment on to us. The teachers who loved learning, loved teaching, loved the kids and thought our ideas were worth listening to—their subjects I never forgot!"

My son's comments brought to mind so many of my own experiences in school: teachers who inspired me; teachers who opened doors to growth and discovery; teachers who helped me to learn more about my world and myself; teachers who showed me the gifts I had to give and the ways in which I might be of service; teachers who filled me with joy; teachers who pushed my mind to a deeper capacity to see the truth and my heart to a more open and compassionate understanding; teachers who brought out in me a desire to help, in some small way, to alleviate suffering and contribute to my world.

I remembered, as well, the classes that bored and discouraged me, the ones that turned me away from subjects, perhaps forever, by reason of the fear instilled in me by a negative teacher. One comes to mind: an English teacher I had as a high school junior, who so attacked my writing that I did not write for five years. My confidence was all but decimated, and I withdrew, no longer daring to express what I had so desperately longed to share. Thank God, I recovered to become what I dreamed of being—a writer. But I fear others, in similar situations, might not be so lucky. For them, the happy experiences with learning might not outweigh those that discourage and paralyze.

We all want to nourish our children. Educators and parents surely want to inspire young people and bring out the best they have to offer. Few of us wish to bore and depress them, or turn them into robots who merely memorize, without concern for their place in the world. Certainly, we seek fresh, new ideas. We can hardly argue with the notion of bringing out the very best our children have to offer. But how do we do this?

This special book tells us how. With concrete experiences in the classroom, with a practical, step-by-step guideline, it describes how this can be done, simply, magnificently. It tells of young people learning, really learning, in an atmosphere of joy and mutual respect, daring to share with others, daring to make mistakes, daring to try out their ideas, to be creative. We see young people enthusiastic about the notion of learning how things have been done in the past, desirous of making the very best use of our valuable heritage, excited about building on the best of what has been. We see them attempting to solve problems that have never been solved before.

I have heard a wise and holy man say that we are here for one purpose and that is to make this a better world. He believed, as I do, that the fate of the world is in the hands of the children. So, we ask ourselves, what can we do to help the children? How can we open doors for them? How can we help to bring forth the natural wisdom residing within?

Elaine Young's extraordinary book sheds much light on these important questions. I feel strongly about this book. It is inspiring, practical, positive and elucidating. Quite simply, if the precepts and methods described in this book were employed on a wide scale, they would, without question, contribute to the survival of the planet.

Barbara Dana
Author, actress, screenwriter
Westchester County, New York

Preface

When I began to work with Elaine Young, I realized that a unique perspective could be brought to bear on an idea that has been proposed and opposed in education circles for many years. Here was a person who was implementing an important method of teaching, not debating it.

I heard, however, in my conversations with Elaine, some expressions of frustration about administrators. Administrators, she felt, were inhibiting her teaching and, in effect, causing her to use energies that would have been better directed toward planning for the children. I decided that perhaps I could bring an administrator's view to her concerns, and help her either circumvent her adversaries or at least understand their problems. It was important to me that she and her colleagues view what she is doing as practicable and important. I saw in the marriage of our views a novel perspective on an educational practice.

As a superintendent of schools, I acknowledge the influence I have over policy and procedure. I recognize the role I play in enabling classroom teachers to work effectively with their children. I recognize equally the enormously sensitive role Elaine plays as a second grade teacher dealing with children on a day to day basis. This recognition of and insight into our mutual roles and responsibilities has influenced and strengthened our sense of the process. What she proposes should be viewed as a reflection of our joint understanding and experience.

Robert Frelow
Superintendent
Greenburgh Central School District #7
Hartsdale, New York

Contents

I am a
blade of grass

Elaine Young

Introduction

I have always wanted to make children feel good about themselves. It seemed that if I could somehow touch the inside of each child, demonstrate to each one his special qualities, help each to know what his/her talents are, convince them, each one of them, how important they are to me and to others, then most of the battle would be won.

My early childhood did not provide me with that sense of self-worth. I was subsequently, however, raised by surrogate parents who, in a very special way, made me feel important, capable of doing anything I wished to do.

I grew up in an apartment house, one flight up with a fire escape outside my window. I often sat at that window to get a view of the outside world. The window looked out onto Watson Avenue. It was a main thoroughfare. Families gathered on the Avenue in their chairs to sit and watch the children play. I remember that they were all Jewish families. I thought that the whole world was Jewish. I was not allowed to go past the front stoop. My mother and father were afraid that I might get hurt, even though I must have been at least five years old. Sometimes I sat on the stoop and talked to a crippled boy who could also go no farther. I would sit for hours watching the children roller-skate or play ball.

My childhood was full of "nots." I was not to play with the other children. I was not to cross the street alone. I was not to talk to my Aunt Sylvia or my cousin Leslie. The world and the people in it were not to be trusted. No fun. No laughter. Only danger and suspicion.

When I reached school age, my mother walked me across the street. The other side of the street was a magic place. There was an open field strewn with litter and wild weeds. I walked slowly through the field and looked at the broken branches, the rocks, observed the changes that seemed to occur every day. It was the only place I was never told "you can't." I remember its friendliness. I remember the insects that crawled along the debris. I returned each day to see if they were there. I watched them and envied the freedom they had. I hated arriving at the corner on the other side of the field because it meant that my adventures were over.

I attended Public School 93. I wanted to go to the honors school. I had passed the tests and had been accepted, but my mother said that I couldn't go because in order to get there I would have to go to the other side of the Bronx on the subway. I remember walking through my favorite field feeling sorry for myself.

My brothers ran away from home at the ages of 16 and 17. I was 13 years old and too frightened and insecure to flee. Fortunately, that very summer, my parents and I came to a resort hotel in the Catskills for one week. There was a feeling of freedom in the open spaces and I would get up very early to watch Anne, one of the owners, in the kitchen baking. She made bread and cakes by mixing big bags of ingredients. Without any apparent measuring, she poured flour, butter and assorted things into a big stainless steel bowl with a big arm in the middle that twisted and turned. Then Anne would take her own arm and wipe off the side of the steel bowl to make sure everything was mixed well. I began to tease her about her customers not knowing she was putting her hands into everything they ate. She laughed and loved to joke about it. I felt warm and funny. I learned laughter and began to share myself. There was no criticism, only a special time when I could enjoy being me. I liked hearing the stories about the hotel and how it got started.

Though it was completely out of character, my parents allowed me to stay on for the rest of the summer as a counselor for the few children who were there with their parents. That was the first of many summers and vacations that I worked and was treated as another member of the Geller family. Anne was loving and caring and a listener. Max was strong and busy and fair. He was the justice of the peace in this small town, and he solved problems with the wisdom of Solomon. He would talk about politics and people, as he made repairs. I would work and paint right along beside him.

Anne and Max gave me the support system that I had not known before. I was included in grown-up conversations and made to feel I had good ideas. I was encouraged to participate and think. I was forced to make choices. Anne and Max would point out alternatives—the benefits and burdens associated with each. What I felt and learned with Anne and Max was that I was perfect the way I was. It was all right to be me. I could cry and laugh and feel.

It was hard to take that back to my home in the Bronx. I often felt like I lived in two worlds. As I grew older I chose to spend more time with Anne and Max and their family. I felt needed, important, cared about, special and able to do anything I wanted. I knew when I started teaching that I must provide a climate in the classroom to make that happen. I had learned how to love and show respect for children. I knew the difference I could and would make in their lives. When children know that they are perfect with me just the way they are, they're then freed up to become whatever they can—just the way I was.

My escape from home came when I started teaching at the age of 20. I was offered a job only fifteen minutes from my home at the Heathcote School in Scarsdale. I did not wish to live or work near my home. I refused the position and took my first teaching job in Bay Shore, Long Island, a fifty-minute car ride away. This gave me the excuse to live away from home. Several years later, after my teaching and continued support from Anne and Max gave me the courage and self-confidence, I returned to Scarsdale for six years.

At Bay Shore, I taught for three years. The first year, I taught a class of 38 "bright" second graders. I remember being frustrated by them. They had been told they were the best. They vied for leadership in the group and seemed more interested in leading than learning. I believed that an important feature of leading was listening to others and becoming a leader through influence and cooperation rather than control and coercion. While that first year was a difficult one, I was convinced that an important aspect of my orientation for the following year would be how I could deal with the personal relationships between and among the children.

I did not get a chance to try out my ideas with the "bright" group. The next year, I was assigned to a group of 35 "slow" second graders. They truly were lacking in the basic skills. I felt that I could improve their skills if I could get their attention. They fought frequently among themselves. They teased and cursed each other. I decided to try to get them to deal with their arguments and fighting by forcing them to sit down and talk about their disagreements. Almost intuitively, I developed a process which worked. The process essentially was to listen to their interpretations of the problem and insist upon their attempting to identify other solutions. The process worked so well that I incorporated it into every feature of the classroom that I could imagine. Problem solving became central to my teaching. I used it not only to deal with social issues, but with academic questions as well. I observed improvement in both.

I did not like the control that individuals in the "bright" group sought to exert over each other and myself. It was exhausting and often frustrating to manage. I equally was not eager to teach a group with a preponderance of problems. It, too, was exhausting and frustrating. I decided that I might reach the children and be more effective if I had an academically and behaviorally diverse group. Perhaps then the interpersonal problems could be better managed. I asked the principal to allow me and a colleague to select such a group. He agreed. The experiences of that year led to my current professional orientation to heterogeneous grouping.

I left Bay Shore at the end of the third year. I did learn, subsequently, that the number of heterogeneous groups have been extended to one class per grade level. Perhaps, in some unconscious way, that affirmed my beliefs.

The experience that really refined my teaching philosophy took place the following September. I was hired to teach second grade in the New Paltz State Teachers College experimental school. Concurrently, I taught a seminar on language arts and a seminar on teaching techniques. The seminars provided the forum for me to evaluate my teaching philosophy. Students from my seminars would observe me teach and would, subsequently, question me in the seminars. They usually asked how I was able to work with small groups and still manage to maintain control of the rest of the class. The question was a significant one. I cannot recall any formal training experience which taught me that skill. I think I taught myself because I cared so much.

I experienced school in my youth as a place where the teacher stood in front of the room and rarely spoke to anyone personally. It seemed just like home. My own classroom, therefore, provided an opportunity for me to give the children the personal attention and decision-making opportunities that I felt all children should have and that sadly I had missed until my days with Anne and Max. I arranged my classroom to maximize personal contact with the children. I used that contact to listen and hear them.

Eventually, the questions my college students asked me caused what was an intuitive approach to become a conscious one. I realized that there was something in me that said, "I need to hear them." I'm not sure exactly when listening, developing interests and problem solving turned into a conscious system for learning. I only know that each year now, as a second grade class, we are able to consolidate our individual interests into a single theme, chosen by consensus, from which all our learning emerges.

Several years ago I tried to outline my thematic approach to learning in the form of a tree. The roots were made of trust and personal regard. The trunk represented our theme, from which branches extended—math, reading, science, social studies.

When I first began this book, I couldn't decide whether to begin with the roots or the branches! Now I see it doesn't matter. All our learning is intertwined. Our thoughts and investigations move back and forth through the leaves like the wind.

Unlike the wind, though, our learning is not capricious but planned.

Elaine Young
2nd Grade Teacher
Purchase School
Harrison Central School District
Harrison, New York

CHAPTER 1

Setting the Stage

I believe that our children will be involved, participating adults who will make a difference in the quality of their own and all our lives. To care about themselves and others, they have to see that the problems in the classroom, as in life, are ones they can own. They are responsible for what they do in the classroom and in life, and they are not alone. By giving and being able to ask for help, they can make a difference. Just knowing that keeps them growing and learning.

I don't believe, though, that this kind of learning is accidental. Teaching is a purposeful, deliberate activity that promotes growth. My teaching begins before the school year starts. Pre-planning provides the climate and sets the stage for the experience of caring, sharing interests and learning from the very first day of school.

I begin with the children. It would be ideal if I had available on each child assigned to my class observations over several years. In the absence of such information, I go to the cumulative folders with the new class list. I review standardized tests to look for areas of outstanding abilities or needs, and note test results. I record parents' occupations for possible resources, and I read teacher's comments.

I find the most meaningful information comes from the former teacher. The information is meaningful even when it is sometimes expressed negatively. I have found, for example, that my colleagues occasionally characterize a child as a "loud mouth" or more usually "boisterous" or "aggressive." Even though I may reject these judgments as negative or subjective, I accept the behavior patterns viewed by the teacher as more or less accurate, and I look for possible reasons for them. I ask teachers to describe work habits, such as taking directions, time-on-task and independence. I ask them if the children have friends in the group from previous classes. When I question the former teachers, I look for a pattern of group dynamics: where they perceive the leadership to be and whether it is positive or negative.

Last year I listened to the first grade teachers describe my prospective class as a disaster. Comments were, "They are so young and immature. They don't listen. If I were going to have a baby this would be the year to take off. It's one of those groups that will be a problem all the way through, just like the present fifth grade class was. I wonder what was in the air the year those children were born."

My thoughts went back to the year I taught that present fifth grade, which was the year we studied insects. What an exciting year that turned out to be! The preliminary comments were similar. The names of the children were different. I realized I needed some positive responses to create the energy I count on when I begin the year.

I began calling the parents during the summer. My goal was to say hello, begin a relationship, show my interest in the children and invite them to bring in examples of their interests the first day of school. I started with the parent of a former student. I needed a supportive first call. Ryan's mother was delighted that I had called. She said Ryan couldn't wait for me to be his teacher. She wanted me to know right away that he was different from his brother. She told me, "He loves music and listens to records all of the time. He loves to draw; he loves poetry and the arts. He is not into sports like his brother." She promised to bring Ryan to visit after camp one day.

I felt a burst of enthusiasm and called Jay's mother. She said, "I want you to know that Jay is a storyteller. He likes to exaggerate. There was a mouse in my neighbor's basement and it became a family of mice that invaded our house when the story got to school. He is a talker and I am told he is constantly talking out. I don't think that comes from the family, since we listen to Jay."

Jay's mother let me know immediately that her son likes to bring things to school. She said, "I hope you won't think he brings too many things in." I assured her that would be great. She said, "Jay is an animal lover. He loves dogs. He has so many plant experiments." I said I would set aside a part of our science table just for him.

Corey's father's first comment was, "Lucky you, you'll earn your money this year." When I asked him to tell me about Corey he said, "He has good days and he has bad days. He is quiet and sensitive. . .You can yell at him and he will never blink an eye. He feels like an outsider. He shows little reaction to anything." I began to feel pain associated with his father's comments. When he told me that his son liked baseball my thoughts went immediately to my own son's friend whose father is the Commissioner of Baseball. I thought, "I will use that connection to reach Corey."

Karie's mother described her daughter as liking to read and do math. "Her satisfaction is in completing tasks, and being responsible, organized, meticulous and orderly." She wondered if Karie would function as well in my class as her brother had because she likes to be told what to do and then approved of for doing it. When I asked about Karie's interests, she said, "Karie has four Cabbage Patch dolls and maybe she could bring them in."

My next call to Matthew's father elicited the following comments: "You have to keep him busy; I like to know what his weaknesses are. Are you structured or open?" I shifted the conversation to the father's experience as a teacher. He told me that he used to be a lawyer but wanted time for his family. He went into teaching so that he could be home early. He said, "I don't send my son to camp because I want to teach him my values so he isn't influenced by others." I knew that both parents were teachers and asked how they spent their summers. He told me they took Matthew to Europe last summer and they had lots of slides of Europe. The father rides his bike 40 miles a week and takes his son out for a few miles a day. The enthusiasm in his voice when he spoke about biking led me to encourage his talking about his working this summer with disabled children in what he described as a deprived area in the Bronx. I asked him to encourage Matthew to bring in any special finds from their biking trips. He said, "I'll see." He ended with the statement, "It's like a little empire in there, and only one king, the teacher."

Caitlin's mother was hesitant on the telephone. She told me that her daughter read a lot. When I asked her what books interested her she said, "Girl books. You know, not the ones that are about sports and the things boys like." They had just been to Montauk and Caitlin had saved some of the fish bones. Her mother explained they smelled. I said, "Just soak the bones in Clorox and the smell will go away," remembering an experience with Karie's brother, Sam, and his bones. Her mother said she threw them out already. She then said, "I will ask Caitlin what her interests are. Often my perceptions of interests are different from hers." I said I would be delighted to have Caitlin call me during the summer.

Natalie's mother told me that she likes swimming, dancing and drawing. Her mother let me know that she teaches dance at a local community house.

Stephanie's father at first told me that she liked to read and do math. He then asked, "Do you know my daughter? Have you seen her?" I said, "No, I have not." He then said, "Stephanie is the child who looks different. She has had eight operations since birth when her skull didn't close. She is missing three fingers and has no toes on one foot." When he finished describing Stephanie's major surgery procedure there was a pause. My response was, "Thank you. I do remember Stephanie now. In the first grade play, at the end of the year she did a wonderful job. How confident she appeared on stage." I was having difficulty using the word "handicap" because it wasn't yet apparent that her condition was handicapping for Stephanie. Stephanie's father continued, "Stephanie doesn't like hospitals. She is well received by her friends and classmates at school, but she is attending a day camp at the other end of town where the children do not know her, and they are making fun of her hands and looks." He then told me that the first grade teacher said Stephanie had tested very well in kindergarten but didn't do as well as she could have. The teacher said that Stephanie cared more about people than her studies. I told him that I would check with the teacher, look at the test results he spoke about and review them with him after school began. I reassured him that for many six and seven year olds socializing is very important.

The conversation became less tense and shifted; I asked him what he did in his job with the New York Department of Transportation. I discovered that he had some very old maps relating to where and how the roads and parkways were developed. He was anxious to locate them and share them with my new class. I was very excited about this and let him know how that would help the children's learning. He then told me that he would have Stephanie call me. She did call the next day and we talked about her coming trip to Lake George and the possibilities of the interests she could bring in to school. She giggled when I told her her father was going to talk to the class and show his maps.

Randy's mother began by saying, "I want to tell you a few of his problems. Randy is a young second grader and I've been told that December boys tend to be immature. He has been tested a lot. He tested well in kindergarten. His penmanship is superb, his work is excellent and his conduct leaves a little bit to be desired. He shouts out. He disturbs other people in the class." I reassured her and described my process of developing trust with the sharing of interests. She said, "That's just what he needs. I am so glad you called. Randy likes building with blocks and he likes to watch TV all of the time. His father is responsible for putting TV shows on the air and he is always watching TV." She then said, "Would you talk to my husband? He relates better to my son than I." I encouraged Randy's father to tell me about his work and I got excited about the possibility of learning how to do animation. He told me that Randy likes to play soccer, likes to do things with his hands, is hyperactive, likes to bounce around a lot and has a low frustration level.

As promised in our original phone call, Ryan's mother brought him to my house after a day at camp. He walked in carrying his younger sister of 14 months and his writing book from first grade. We took a walk in my backyard—Ryan, his sister and me. He showed a real affection and concern for Ruth. He had a third ear and eye for her, yet it never stopped his talking to me. He was so proud of his writing. He told me his stories were about animals—the ones they studied about in first grade. I told Ryan I like to write and he looked at my typewriter and piles of paper. I asked him if he would like to write stories and not have them corrected. He responded, "No—I want the words spelled right." He then shared his strong feeling about wanting a pet dog. I asked him why he wanted to come to my class. He said, "My brother said you didn't give a lot of homework and I don't want lots of homework." After our walk, Ryan offered to write some more stories for me during the summer. I shared my excitement about that and didn't make any suggestions about the topics.

I went inside to get Ryan's mother. When she and I got to the car, Ryan's fingers were full of grease from playing around with the door latch. I said, "Don't worry, we can wash that off." Ryan and I went into the kitchen. I put both of our hands under the faucet, and as I started to use the Comet cleanser, the grease went from his fingers to mine. He giggled. He said, "You look like a grease monster." I laughed out loud and asked Ryan to write one of his stories about me as a Grease Monster. His immediate response was, "No, I can't do that." I left it alone. When we got back outside, the car door latch was now jammed so that the door would not close. I got a screwdriver and Ryan's mother moved it partially. I asked Ryan to compare the other door latch to see which way it turned. His mother was getting frustrated and I went for a rope to tie the door at the window frame. With everyone in the car I then said, "Ryan, what a great adventure story this would make. Will you write it for me?" He replied, "Oh no, my dad will get mad." Ryan's mother didn't say anything and I waved goodbye.

These encounters, the vignettes I remember, become an integral part of my planning. My challenge is how to use them in setting up the classroom. I have many materials I have accumulated over the years, but I want to keep an open mind about what might stir children's interests. So I consciously decide to limit what I bring to the class because

I want them to participate in the building of the classroom environment. Even so, I begin with quite a collection.

I have generally found my seven year olds uninterested in reading. Some of them will not even pick up the picture books that I place around the room. A few confide to me that they don't like books, and I know they don't know how to read. I plan my book display, therefore, so that children experience the joy, adventure and excitement of books. I select some books for the room library that I will read to them, and some that the children will be able to read themselves without difficulty. My objective at the outset is not to develop vocabulary or raise reading levels, but to excite my students about the world of books.

There is another world I want to excite them about as well. We sometimes refer to it as the "real world." The real world is commonly viewed as anything outside of the classroom. To overcome that handicap I bring myriad objects and items into my room. I spend two or three weeks each year prior to the opening of school assembling ordinary items that are seen every day in the children's surroundings. My selections are representative of both the natural and the manufactured world. I collect rocks from the pathways and playgrounds. I collect leaves and twigs, branches, bark, bugs and blossoms from the parks and parkways. I collect bottles and boxes, spools, threads, yarns, ropes, cloth of various colors and textures, cereal boxes, balls, buttons, pins, pens, postage stamps, playing cards, baseball cards, I. D. cards, credit cards, post cards. I also bring in newspapers, magazines, journals, catalogs, trade books, classic paintings, children's painting from previous classes, photographs and picture puzzles. All of my treasures have been donated by parents, publishers and local merchants or confiscated from attics, basements and unkempt closets.

My search for materials is systematic. I look for items that might excite the children's interest visually, through color, shape, size and form. I appeal to their sense of touch through strength, malleability and texture. I want the children to associate the items with familiar territory—their homes, playgrounds, parks, museums and libraries. We need the unfamiliar too, so as to arouse curiosity about origin, composition and application. I want to prepare for the variety of ways children learn.

This year, I walked into my room the first day of August. The custodians were not there yet, so I could just look around and match the room with the group as it was emerging in my mind. I glanced at my favorite corner. That space has been used in so many different ways depending on the year and the children—a display table, a catch all, a special place for talking, an area for designing a book, a play-writing workshop, a layout table or my private typing and thinking area. The year that we studied insects, we wrote a very factual insect guide in that space. During the superstition year, we created a fun-filled fantasy called "Narnia Newspaper."

The corner is next to what I have come to call the math area. It most often becomes a place for children to build with Cuisenaire rods, geometric blocks and pattern blocks. Over the years I have learned to put out the math materials that lend themselves to building. That's the first place for problems to arise and the place that the children have heard about from brothers and sisters and friends. When they ask "Can we build with the rods?" I tell them they will talk about it and set up a pattern for using the math corner. I need to observe what they see as problems and solutions to problems. Since I was told this was a difficult class with aggressive children, I knew the math corner would be a good test of how they handle problems. I walked around the room musing to myself.

"I will set aside time the first day to see what problems develop. The children have had the lid put on them alot. I need to be careful about how much to let go so I don't change their pattern too abruptly. I want to have control without having to raise my voice. I will put pictures of former children working together on the bulletin board. It shows them smiling and cooperating."

I consider the nature of the group as a whole, but most especially I want to relate my materials to what I already know about individual students. I think of the children as I arrange my room.

"I just completed a workshop on word as image in art. I became fascinated with Jackson Pollack and how I read the pattern in his art. I will look for a picture and put it up with the three key words that it evoked for me. One of my images was of dance. That will be a connection for Natalie. Dance is not one of my best areas. Perhaps I can get movement poems or paintings of dancers."

My thoughts went to Ryan and the Grease Monster story. "He likes writing, drawing, music and poetry. I can bring in Erica Ross records. She uses the guitar and is a story teller. I will invite Sandy the librarian to tell a story with a picture book. Maybe the first day. I have never had a visitor the first day."

"Jay is the storyteller, who also loves sports. I will collect baseball action pictures. They'll be great for story telling. I'll use Jay to begin. The Mets are winning. We'll remember to call Tommy Valentine's father, the Commissioner of Baseball. I need to involve Corey somehow."

"Stephanie's father has Hutchinson River Parkway maps. I will get some of the maps to hang up for the first day of school. I can tie in trips taken by children during the summer, using their road maps. Will there be enough bulletin board space? I'll need to solve that problem this year."

"Matthew likes biking and the Olympics. This was the first year women competed in bicycling at the Olympics." My thoughts go to competition; sports and cooperation. "I will have to get books and pictures about bicycles and biking. There are only four girls in the class. That will please Caitlin, who likes girl books. The books show that girls can do boy things."

"Randy watches TV. We should discuss children's TV watching habits. Perhaps Randy and his parents can show us the usefulness that can occur in watching TV critically. Once we made a videotape with parents and children on TV."

"While I was watching the news on TV, a reporter was describing a doll exhibit in Soho at the Eclipse Gallery. The dolls are collectable toys, artwork that ranges from $500 to $5000. I will call the woman from the SUNY Art Workshop I attended, to have her bring her puppets into the class. I will call Van Craig, one of the doll exhibitors, to talk to the class. He lives in New York and uses a commercial form of paper mache. This is a connection for Karie and her Cabbage Patch Dolls.''

Out of this hodgepodge of interests and artifacts will emerge a single connecting theme, arrived at by the children, which will provide the focus for all their learning. I never know in advance what the theme will be. I remember the year I was sure the children were headed toward a cross between wood and Indian lore, and we ended up with superstitions. In the insect year, we started off with a garbage fascination.

Involving parents, even in the pre-planning stage, makes the theme develop faster. I hope to promote trust and enthusiasm, which leads to student interaction and involvement. I'm looking for a rapport, so that parents can feel safe about sharing a piece of home at school. Trust and enthusiasm translate themselves into a respect for children as they are, not as we would like them to be some time in the future. Parents can recognize and support the interests developing in their children and discover the direct and indirect relationships between their own and their childrens' interests. That frees children to explore the connections within the classroom.

Because I want the children to have the opportunity to discover for themselves the materials of the "outside world" and participate in the building of the classroom environment, I consciously leave areas of the room barren in an effort to prompt them to bring in items of their own interest. I have found that until there is a climate of trust between teacher and children this is a tenuous expectation.

CHAPTER 2

Building Trust

F rom the very first day of school, the children want to show me who they think they are. They have begun to believe the roles that have characterized their actions for years.

I observe and record as much as I can that first day to see if the children play the roles as they have been described to me. How they behave will tell me how they feel about themselves. They exhibit characteristics I've heard attributed to them by teachers, parents or in case conferences. They describe themselves as others describe them. Children act out the roles assigned to them by others.

When I read my notes of the comments of previous teachers and then read my anecdotal records for that first day experience, I see consistent similarities:

1) Previous teacher's description—"aggressive."

My description—"Wanted to be first in line."

2) Previous teacher's description—"bossy."

My description—"Had many suggestions about the way the day should go."

3) Previous teacher's description—"quiet, shy."

My description—"Waited to see what was going on before venturing out."

The possibility also exists, though, that describing the children's behavior anecdotally, rather than descriptively, will introduce potential differences between my observation and those of the previous teacher. The opportunity is created for the child to change, to grow and develop rather than be "stuck" in a particular behavior.

1) Previous teacher's description—"quiet, reserved."

My description—"Surveyed the situation, analyzed from a distance the teacher, peers, room parameters, and his/her responsibilities."

2) Previous teacher's description—"friendly."

My description—"Smiled despite circumstances."

3) Previous description—"nervous, anxious, tense."

My description—"Constantly asks 'Are we going to get a book today? How do you grade? Will I get an 'A' on my report card?'"

4) Previous description—"In a fog, daydreamer."

My description—"Had an unusual idea."

At the end of the day, I have an anecdotal record on every child for the first day. I record what the children have said and how I felt about what was said. How I feel about the children's behavior is crucial to how I respond to them. I pay particular attention to my negative responses to specific behaviors. I tend to be put off initially by the so-called "noisy, bossy" children who early in the game announce their intention not to be guided by any of the rules. After a while, when it becomes clear that this behavior is the child's way of getting my attention, I merely give it to them and they become convinced they can have it without such behavior.

I am more persistently concerned about the children who appear frightened and attempt to fade into the background. I'm upset particularly if there appears to be no change in these children's observable behaviors or at least the teacher's evaluation of that behavior since their arrival in school.

The hardest job is to decide how to relate to these children. Sara was a very shy child. I find my inclination is to tune in to the shy child first. I'm very cautious, but I make sure that I make some physical contact with shy children—a touch on the arm, the shoulder, the head—on a daily basis. Sara always wore pretty dresses. "Sara, that's such a pretty dress. Can I touch it?" Initially I attempt to communicate without imposing any work-oriented tasks. I don't want to associate myself yet with "teacher work" while I try to communicate.

I have found that children who are generally characterized as "shy" react well to fantasy and have vivid imaginations. All of the children are given a notebook which I call their record book. The record book is a "record" of their writings and drawings. I soon discovered Sara could express her feelings in writing, usually in fantasy form. Sara wrote, in a single year, four record books of stories, poems and drawings. She developed tremendous pride in her record books, a pride that was shared by me and her parents. She was not content from that point on to confine her writing to herself and her record book. She felt the room should have a "writing corner" where stories and poems by all the children would be created and shared. I agreed.

Sometimes children are not ready to assume the responsibilities adults confer upon them. They are so used to merely acceding to the directions and decisions of others that they are uncomfortable with situations where they are given choices and required to make decisions.

My immediate challenge the first day of school is to convince the children that they really do have choices. Most of the children are used to having their seats assigned to them and experience considerable discomfort when they discover that there is no specific place for them to sit. The children have already noticed that the seating arrangements are unfamiliar. I must, therefore, provide a familiar context to orient them to my style of teaching. I assemble them immediately in what we have come to call "the discussion circle" where the children sit in a circle at the center of the room—usually on the floor.

A typical conversation ensues:

"Where do we sit, Mrs. Young?"

"There are several places you may choose to work," I respond.

"But we don't know what to do. The teacher usually tells us where to sit."

"Would you like to try not being told?" I ask. "If we have problems then we'll sit down together and see if we can work them out."

On the first day I tell the children that the seating "problem" is one example of the many special situations that develop in the classroom. Time, I explain, will be set aside regularly for something called "problem solving." We will discuss the issues until they are narrowed down to the simplest expression of what is contributing to the conflict. I let them know that they will be given all the assistance possible, but it's their responsibility to work out solutions. I will assist them with the process, which usually includes stating the problem, brainstorming as many alternative solutions as can be suggested by the group and finally agreeing on one of those alternatives. Our first newsletter illustrates the beginnings of that process.

Sept. 5, 19—

Dear Parents,

We would like to share some of our exciting beginnings. We hope you will use our newsletters to talk with your child about their interests and their participation in our second grade.

We chose our cubbies and our seats. Many interesting alternatives were suggested and a choice was easily agreed upon. We have two cabinets with 24 cubbies altogether. There are 12 cubbies in each cabinet.

Matthew suggested we use 7 cubbies in one cabinet and 7 cubbies in the other cabinet. There are 14 children in the classroom. Caitlin suggested that the girls get one cabinet and the boys get the other. Esther said we could take one any place.

The class agreed to have the girls use one cabinet and the boys the other cabinet. Ryan said, "Since most of the boys are near the back, let's use that one." They agreed.

I am excited about the wonderful stories and pictures that have been started in our record books. Your child might like to keep a special diary at home.

We will be learning more about our interests. Here is our first interest chart. If you have anything related to our interests, please send it in with your child or call Mrs. Young.

ANIMALS		MAPS
tigers		Israel
camels		Iran
lions	ROADS	
giraffes		bicycles
pandas		
	dinosaurs	dolls
	shells	
	money	

Mrs. Young's Second Grade Class

When I insist that children choose their own place to work, select their own cubbies, draw with a new variety of materials, look at a picture with which they are familiar and compare it with another artist, get a sense of excitement and joy out of pursuing their interests and discovering new ones, I am having children practice the skills of questioning, problem solving, listening to others, testing solutions and stretching their minds.

As the first newsletter indicates, we are also beginning our quest for a theme by identifying and trying to gather our interests. Problem solving, developing interests and learning are related and sequential.

What I cannot tell the children is the strong feelings that will develop around these class problems and how they ultimately become the primary source of trust-building in the classroom.

"He took my seat!"

"I don't want that girl next to me."

"I want to sit next to Mary!"

They begin to express their feelings to me right away. Some are angry. Others are intimidated. Some just sit and wait to see what I'm going to do. They soon discover that they can express their real fears (which usually turn out to be related to the choices they will have to make every day) and I will not get angry with them! When the children realize that I accept their feelings as valid, when they realize that other children feel the same as they, when they realize that the teacher has set up a process where their feelings are asked for and received with support and encouragement by the other children, then the bond of trust has developed and I can teach them.

Adam's father was a prominent surgeon, his mother a lawyer. His older brother was identified as a gifted child. Adam wasn't reading as well as his parents would have liked. He often fought with his brother. He said, "My brother comes into my room and takes my things and gets me in trouble with my mother and father. They always believe him and I get punished." I invited the parents in. The father met me one morning at 7:00 A.M. before going to the hospital. He related a story about how he punished Adam for fighting with his brother. He removed all of the furniture in his room except his bed.

Adam's anger was so great he wouldn't yell, he would bite. He felt picked on. If anything happened, it wasn't he who was doing anything, it was somebody doing something to him. He was academically oriented, but not achieving at the level of genius, like his brother. He had potential, but was blocked by emotional needs. He constantly brought attention to himself.

Adam came in to school the day after he lost his furniture telling me what all of the children in the class were doing to him. He was so anxious to tell his side of the story that he found it difficult to listen and kept interrupting. We had just come back from gym and some of the children were on line in the hallway getting a drink of water. Someone pushed in front of Adam. He took the child's arm and bit into it. He was so angry that I had to hold him. Adam found it hard to listen to the other child's side of the story, but gradually he found that when both sides were listened to, it meant that he was listened to and taken seriously. He began to calm down.

When Adam's dog died, Adam was very upset, because the dog was his "friend." The whole class sat and listened while he poured out his sorrow. He mourned verbally all day. He poured out his thoughts in his writing and illustration. He knew that I admired his stories and illustrations.

In this classroom, he found that emotions were respected and dealt with—in discussion over conflict and in creative expression. With the study of insects, Adam's intellectual interest was expressed emotionally. He expressed affection for the insects. When Flyer, our butterfly, escaped from his cage, Adam was so connected that he knew exactly what to do.

In that same year, the insect year, Johnny told about going down to the pond in back of his house and catching a frog with Randy. He related the details about squeezing the frog to death, and how its guts were coming out. Some of the children saw nothing wrong with that. Others told Johnny how weird and awful it was. He smiled and really liked the attention he was getting from the story. He also liked getting some of the children upset. I asked Johnny why he did it. He answered that there were so many frogs that they weren't important.

We had been studying about insects and I began to talk about the chain of life and how everything was important—frogs eating the insects and other animals eating the frogs. Hal related how there were frogs in the swamp land while his house was being built and now they were gone. I knew Johnny's mother was involved in a course on ecology at Manhattanville College. I told Johnny that I was going to ask his mother to invite her teacher to speak to our class. Ms. Harris from Manhattanville came to our class two days later with Johnny's mother. She talked about water pollution in the local ponds and rivers and the effect on insects and animals, and what happened when bulldozers filled in places where insects and frogs lived. We began collecting insects after Ms. Harris left.

The boy who squeezed a frog caught a cricket three weeks into school—during recess. Johnny carefully brought it into the class and put it in a jar. I asked the children if they wanted to keep the cricket in the classroom. These same children who saw nothing wrong with killing a frog said, "We can't do that, it would die without food." I asked if they wanted to let it go at three o'clock. "No," they emphatically said, "It won't have any air in the closed jar. Let's let it go now." So they did, with such a feeling of pride and caring.

I gave Johnny the job of finding out about the parts of a cricket. I made a cricket and insect chart for him. I then told him he was the expert and knew more than the rest of the class about crickets. Even though Johnny was a nonreader, he could read the chart to the rest of the class, and did, with pride.

At the end of the year, when the class learned about handicapped kids who were going to be mainstreamed the next year, the children said, "They may look different, and not act like us but they have feelings." Johnny said, "I'll break the head of anybody who doesn't know that those kids have feelings like the rest of us."

Caring is important in our classroom. Johnny was the first one who ran to look for Meg's poetry when she was upset about losing it. Johnny stopped getting headaches when he picked up a book by December. His drawings changed from crayon mushes called Star Wars to insects by February or March, and he began to read during May and June. He scored a 2.5 grade level in reading in April, from a 1.2 at the end of first grade.

There is a parallel between personal and intellectual development. As there is growth and freedom in one, so there is in the other. The balance is essential, and it is a never-ending back and forth process, nourishing the spirit and nourishing the mind.

I never fail to be excited and a little surprised when it happens once again. A child grows before my eyes when he is cared for and responded to with honesty and warmth.

This year, the children were enjoying writing in their record books. As they began to realize that what they wrote or drew was fine with me, they began to share. Our morning discussions often presented a pattern and ideas for their writing. We read poetry every morning and Shel Silverstein was a favorite. The poem, "Us," has a funny line that uses the word "pee." The children insisted that I read it every morning and we all got hysterical. After the first reading of the poem, Jeremy began drawing pictures of female and male anatomy, explicitly showing the figures and writing in the word "pee."

Jeremy up to that point was unwilling to stick to a task. One morning as we shared our writing and pictures, he showed the pictures that he had made in his record book. To his surprise, instead of laughter, Karie responded with "That's disgusting. Other people don't want to hear junky stuff. Shel Silverstein is funny—that isn't." Several of the boys and girls agreed about how his pictures and descriptions made them feel. Jeremy got very quiet. He listened carefully. He did not seem to take what they said in an angry way. He let them say it and, rather than respond, just left it alone. He did not need to defend himself and saw that they were truly listening to his sharing. The very next day Jeremy wrote a poem that he shared and the children applauded. He began to complete assignments for me right after that and became involved with two other boys in making a music book. He was freed up to learn by knowing that he could share and be responsible for his sharing, because the children were interested in him and liked him— not his silliness. He asked for a new record book and the quality of his writing changed. He was much less interruptive.

Coby spent the first two weeks of school not moving from his seat, not talking to anyone when we were working in the classroom, drawing and not beginning to write anything associated with his pictures, not choosing to participate. When the pattern of the lunch room changed, the children complained about the change. This was the first time Coby shared. He said "They tell you when to get milk and ice cream. I used to get it when I got everything ready to eat. I don't like that."

By the end of the week, Coby had made three pictures of a sun, a house and a tree. I kept inviting him to share his pictures. The praise from the children followed each sharing. By the end of the second week Coby wrote a poem.

COBY'S POEM

The Sky said
The Sun is warm
The Tree said
The Sun is hot
The House said
The Sun is cold
And
The Sun said
I'm PERFECT.

The round of applause when he read his poem evoked the first broad smile on his face. The poetry began to flow and his mother came to school to tell me that during the long weekend off, Coby wanted to know when it was going to be Monday. "I wish I could go to school now." He now walks in with a big smile. He is walking all around the room, standing over the children to see what they are doing and asking to be a part of things. He built a structure with the rods. He asks questions when our visitors come in. He even gets a little lost in what he is doing and waits for me to call him a second time. He is involved in learning with the other children and is happier at the tasks he chooses or is given. He will more often work at different places, rather than just sitting at one seat all day. He's testing everything.

Karie and Caitlin like to be perfect. They believe that everything and everyone in the classroom reflect on them. They had a problem with Randy. Randy came into the room one morning in tears.

He said "Every time, Karie and Caitlin make fun of me, when I get off the bus and on the playground. They whisper to each other about me."

Karie and Caitlin responded, "We don't like him, he bothers us a lot with the sounds he makes."

"They mimic me and stick their tongues out."

"If people walk in our room, they won't like us when they see Randy sticking out his tongue and making clicking noises."

"They're imitating me."

I asked Randy, "How does it help you to do that?"

He said, "Because I like to do it. It's fun to do it."

Karie said, "Mrs. Young, you don't send him out of the room." They were unable to come to any agreement and I asked if we could present the problem to the class. They agreed.

Stephanie said, "He has a habit. Let's give him help with his habit. Make a habit chart."

Matthew said, "He will keep his word if he promises to stop. He has before. Make him promise."

Karie said, "One time of the day, make him stop."

Natalie said, "You don't want to get mad at him."

Matthew and Ryan said, "Let us try."

The two boys took Randy into the math corner and included him in their building. Matthew said, "All we did was work with him and he didn't make the noises. Nobody was working with him or listening when he said something. It's more fun to do this than shout at him."

Randy said, "It made me feel better."

The boys discovered, "We listened to him and he listened to us and he didn't have to make those noises."

The very arrangement of the room prepares the children for choice-oriented learning. Ready-to-learn means that they will be willing to take an active role in what they will learn. They come in wanting to know how many pages they have to do; whether I will give a star or a smiling face when they finish their work. I have to reassure them. The transition cannot be too abrupt or so alien that the children see no relationship to their previous school experiences. I assure them that they will have readers and workbooks and I will use them at a pace that is comfortable. They are made aware of the daily patterns of work which include paper and pencil work at their seats.

Immediately reassured, they begin to take risks. The arrangement of the room itself and the kind of materials that are placed around brings them to ask, "When can I touch the things on the science table?" "Who gets to use the clay?" "What are all those games?" I carefully select the amount of materials and the materials themselves to provide immediate problem solving situations.

September 7, 19—

Dear Parents,

Caitlin said, "We always solve problems in our classroom and everything works out all right." Matthew said that we solve problems when we ask questions. The problem is what we do. We have to make a choice.

Ryan and Jay said there was a problem today. Ryan said "We want to use the pattern blocks and Barry built on and on with the pattern blocks and kept it up for three days."

Matthew said, "There are still more pattern blocks."

Jay said, "There still won't be enough."

Barry said, "But I want to keep it up and take some parts and make it bigger."

Jay said, "Wreck half of it."

Caitlin said, "Split them up and some get half and some get the other half."

Karie said, "They could make a big building together."

Corey said, "They could keep it up for three days each."

Natalie said, "Barry can finish what he is building and then the other two can do what they want."

Jay, Barry and Ryan chose to split it in half. When Jay and Ryan started to work together, they made a yellow path connecting to Barry's building. Barry made an alligator pit. Jay and Ryan made a kingdom, and the whole thing became a zoo.

Solving problems and choosing will help us to do our work better. Randy said, "You can choose not to bother other people when they are working. It helps me to read a book, learn about things and learn about animals and maps."

Matthew chose to write a story for more than two hours. That broke a record in Mrs. Young's classroom. Matthew said, "I feel good."

Mrs. Young's Second Grade Class

The problems that arose this year in the classroom as a result of my pre-planning involved the use of clay, the use of the Cuisenaire rods in the math corner and a pet rabbit. Future problems will involve assuming responsibility, completing assignments, allotting time, setting priorities and evaluating our own work.

As the children began to work with a limited amount of clay, they shared problems with great feeling. "Not everybody is getting a turn." "We were making something special and other people wanted to use the clay." "What if you're making something big?" "It might break and you may want to do it over."

A typical list of complaints about the use of the Cuisenaire rods ran: "Nobody can use the rods." "When are you going to take it down?" "It's no fair." "Let's wreck it." "We're not done with it." "We want to keep building it." "You'll have to wait." "Why don't you take it down now so that we can start building?" "No, tough luck! We still want to build." "We want to get a picture of it." "I want to go to the bathroom." "Let's talk about it later."

The problems associated with the rabbit sounded like: "Some people are holding her for a long time." "Barbara gets her all the time."

A solution to the triple problems of clay, rods and rabbit was to allow the boys to have the rods and the clay and the girls to have the rabbit. When they tried that and it didn't work, they said, "We need to talk about it again." They began to develop a concern for the animal rather than themselves. "What happens if there is a fire drill?" "The fire bell could scare her." "The cage would be too heavy to carry." "What if she starts to bite because she's afraid?" "How are we going to get the food?" The solutions were: "We could pick her up and take her with us." "You could hold her by the scruff of her neck and keep her away from you." "Mary and Robbie will start, she's used to them."

Some groups have more difficulty finding solutions to sharing. As Laura said, "It takes time to solve problems. Sometimes it doesn't seem like anything's happening but things just get better by talking about them."

Ultimately, as trust develops, the questions, and the problems to be solved, are less "me" oriented. Less concerned with getting their share, being heard or having their way, the children begin to be involved in the real business of education. Now problem solving means sharing and gathering information.

I want the children to be able to read and write, to know the importance it will make in their lives when they do it the best they can, and I let them know that their best can get better. I am asking children to test themselves and be able to own what they do. I insist that they see themselves as thinkers, and I seek to provide an opportunity for them to be deliberate in their thinking. I am asking children to practice solving problems and making connections. This kind of learning is not limited to second grade. It is lifelong and can take place—any place—at any time. There are always connections to be made, new and exciting paths to follow. As Laura says, "It takes time, but it's worth it."

Sharing Feelings

I'd like to tell you about what happened one week in my classroom. It meant a lot to me and clarified much of what I know about connections between trust and interests and feelings and learning.

As a teacher, I have often let children talk to me privately about death. It has always been difficult for me to handle this subject, and I seldom did more than listen and give sympathy. But a classroom incident brought us close to death as a group. We shared our thoughts and feelings about death together and through our experience, I came to terms with a personal loss of my own.

It was during the year my second grade class chose insects as a central theme. As part of our class study, we raised butterflies in captivity in the winter, out of season. In our butterfly litter, a butterfly was born that we all grew to love. We named him Flyer. He had ripped wings, and yet he lived with us through three cold winter months. The children saw Flyer as a courageous friend. They spoke of him often and worried about him.

The last weekend of Flyer's life, I decided not to take him home for the weekend as usual. It had been warm, and it didn't seem necessary.

Unfortunately, the weather turned cold again over the weekend. When we came back to school on Monday morning, the children discovered Flyer dead. I felt terrible and guilty. Suddenly, my own child's death came back to me. After years of blocking out the memory of her death, in the weeks that followed, I kept seeing parallels between her death and that of the butterfly my class had taken to its heart.

Together in our shared need, we wrote the story of Flyer's life and death, and day by day I kept a diary of our work. When the story was done, we felt relieved and fulfilled.

THE DAY BEFORE

I was tired from a late flight home from Florida, yet excited to return to school. Friday evening at the airport, I met seven year old Geoff, who was meeting his brother. We greeted each other with a hug and a kiss. I said, "I miss Flyer—do you?"

"Yes," he answered.

"Can we do anything to remember Flyer?" I wondered out loud.

"I'm going to do one of my special pictures of Flyer," he said.

"What is the one thing that you remember the most about Flyer?" I asked.

"That he died," he answered.

DAY ONE

I sat down in the discussion circle at 9 A.M. Monday morning. All of the children were anxious to tell about their vacations. After the tenth child had spoken, I realized I had heard the buzz of voices, but they didn't make any sense. I wanted to talk about Flyer. Silently I told myself, "Listen to the children. If Flyer's death is not as important to them as it is to you, you mustn't pursue it."

All of a sudden I felt panicked. It was Geoff's turn. Would he remember our words at the airport? When he began to speak, I saw that he did. He re-enacted our whole conversation about Flyer for the rest of the class. The class responded with interest. They seemed to want to remember Flyer in some way. I suggested that we write about Flyer. The children agreed with me that we should write the story together as a class.

I asked the class the same question I asked Geoff—"What is the one thing that you remember about Flyer?"

"That you moved the leaf to see if Flyer was dead," said Marc.

"Flyer died standing up," Bobby said, "the way he was handicapped. His wing was ripped. He was cute, I didn't see how he could live, walk around and fly with a handicapped wing. It was like a miracle."

"He forced himself to stay alive," said Laura. "We helped him by giving him sugar water and taking care of him. We all liked him so."

Tyler said, "Flyer should be mounted and put in a museum."

The children had responded with such intense enthusiasm that I decided to let them go with it. We started where I knew the children were most comfortable—with their drawings. I got out their drawing paper. The discussion group dispersed, and each child went about remembering Flyer in his or her own way—through writing, thinking, looking at Flyer standing in his cage, talking with one another or drawing.

I went from child to child visiting for a moment with each one to sense his or her feelings, to offer encouragement, to look over what each was doing, to help each one to dig deeper into his or her thoughts, observations, writing or drawing.

As I saw the children's work, I began to consider how to develop a group story. But they all had such different things to say about Flyer. I had to be sensitive to the differences in each child's feelings about Flyer and somehow draw them all together.

Meg called me over. She said, "My aunt wrote a book. It had different chapters and different people." Meg went on to suggest that we had read a lot of short books like Beatrix Potter's. I thought, I must find a time today to pull the children together, after they have worked, but when they are still enthusiastic and not yet tired. I wanted to look over the Beatrix Potter books with the children.

Meg thought the class story should follow a structure beginning with how Flyer was born and the life of Flyer, followed by how he died and ending with how we missed him. She said, "Do you know how they have on a book jacket what the story is about in a short way? We could say that we have different people in our class so they all do different things. So there is more than one writer and illustrator. . . ."

About an hour and a half from the time we began working, I called the group together in our library corner. We imagined some foods that only Flyer would have eaten. The children thought of nectar soda, leaf lettuce, and leaf pie a la mode. Meg and Amelia decided they would work together on "Flyer's Fabulous Food Recipes." I thought the idea was very imaginative, and I encouraged the two girls to work on it. I wasn't sure quite where the recipe ideas would fit into Flyer's story or where we would use them, but I encouraged the girls to develop the theme while they felt excited about it.

We had developed a list of character traits for many of the Beatrix Potter characters. I asked the children to do the same for Flyer. They came up with: "liked flying," "liked story time," "nice," "broken wing," "handicapped," "still standing up," "wild," "batting around like crazy," "lived long," "not afraid to die," "never quit," "playing tricks," "strong," "tortuous."

The children discussed possible titles. They liked "The Story of Flyer," "The Adventures of Flyer," "Flyer and His Friends," and "The Sadness of Flyer."

All year we had studied insects, but this was going to be the story of one insect who was very special to the children. When our group broke for lunch, Laura said, "I wish Flyer didn't die." That night I went home with Laura's words in my mind.

DAY TWO

I came in and looked at Flyer, who was still standing in his cage. I remembered the butterfly collection Geoff had brought in and wondered if I could have Flyer mounted. Perhaps the Museum of Natural History could help me out.

When the morning's discussion began, the children's interest in death and stories about the deceased intensified. Three of the children shared personal experiences with death, and as they talked everyone listened quietly.

Adam had met me at the door so excited about somebody he knew who had been killed that his sentences were incoherent, and to this day I do not know who the person was. James, who had just come back from Florida, told us about an alligator he saw that had grabbed a child and kept the boy under water so long that the boy had drowned. Amelia said that a long time ago she had heard about a boy who had fallen into a sewer and died.

Johnny shouted out, "Why do all the boys only have to die?" The other children chimed in. "Yes, why only the boys?"

I said nothing. I was able to say nothing. I began to think of my baby daughter, and my hands started trembling.

The children wanted to begin working. They were interested in continuing their work about Flyer and his death, individually or in small groups. I often post the children's work on a bulletin board, and now I felt a particular need to lose myself in the physical work of setting up the board. I needed time to think and I knew the children would feel special when they saw their work exhibited.

While the children worked, they kept asking me to spell words for them. I made a list of the words they were using in their work. The vocabulary that interested the children included the words color, orange, pattern, wing, formation, examine, science, table, shelf, before, after, chrysalis, emerge, batting around like crazy, loved long, sugar, water, tongue, finger, saved, fly, ripped, dies, wish, mounted, became, and friend.

Meg and Amelia had completed a long list of "Flyer's Fabulous Recipes." I set apart a special section of the bulletin board for them and put them in the order the girls wanted. The children started bringing me some of their pictures. I labeled a part of the board "Flyer Pictures" and put them up. Marc wanted me to take his story of Flyer—which was illustrated—from his record book and put it up. I cut it out and arranged it in the order he wanted. James wanted to have his Flyer drawings exhibited on the bulletin board, but he didn't want them taken from the book where he had drawn them. I realized how much their work on Flyer meant to the children. I resolved to get each one a special, hardcover book to work in and keep for as long as he or she wanted.

By 11 A.M., the children were still working, but I began to get tired. I had been engrossed in working with them, and at the same time trying to keep the most troubling memories of my daughter's death from my mind.

To help us begin writing our group story, we sat down and examined book titles and initial sentences. Which ones made us want to read on? The class decided that children's books usually start out with "Once upon a time," or "One day. . . ." They wanted to start our book with something more interesting.

All of a sudden, Marion said, "No one knew that the only larva on the top was going to be Flyer." We were silent. The children and I knew we had our first sentence. I saw that I should begin the story in the group right then, and we did.

I went to lunch beaming.

After lunch it was story time. I try to read to the children every single day of the school year. The class knew and loved *Where the Wild Things Are*, by Maurice Sendak, and asked to have the story read to them again. I asked them to examine the book as I read it, noting the placement of the words on the page, how Mr. Sendak did the illustrations and what made the book so good.

Meg noticed that Mr. Sendak repeated a pattern throughout the book. Other children noticed that he didn't finish a whole sentence on one page, and there were whole pages without words. Part of the story sounded like part of a poem. The most important words were printed in bigger type. We talked about doing some of the same things in our book.

Our own ideas included putting writing in the pictures and emphasizing certain words by placing them on a page without a picture. Meg said, "Maybe we could end the book with only two words." That fascinated me. What two words?

We concluded our discussion by deciding that we should find a pattern for our book about Flyer. We should include our poetry as part of the story. The children felt our story should be "sad," "happy," "angry," "exciting," "change your mood," "adventurous," "joyful," "brave," "scary," "funny," "beautiful," and I agreed!

I told the children I would keep a record book also. They asked me to share my stories during sharing time. I was afraid to. Should I share my most private feelings about my young daughter's death? Could I become that much a part of the group?

It was time for cleanup. Just before the three o'clock bell, Meg ran over to me with tears streaming down her cheeks. She had lost her poems. "I worked so hard," she said, "and they were so special, and I don't know if I could write them the same way again." As soon as the children heard her, each one searched frantically for her papers. The children's response to Meg's loss surprised and pleased me. Some previous classroom incidents had made me wonder how a teacher can teach compassion to children. Suddenly this was no longer a problem.

A few of the boys spotted Meg's poetry underneath some other papers on the large writing table. Meg dried her eyes. When I read her poetry, I understood why she had been so upset.

I wonder what it would be like
To be a butterfly?
and to fly fly fly fly fly fly
up to the sky
and take a piece of cloud
and feel it
Of course I'm just
a butterfly
I can't soar up
so high
so if I cannot do that
I have to say
GOOD-BYE

Flyer was a
butterfly that made our lives

stand still
he made us
like the sound
of tearing wings
but then came the day
we feared it would come
The day when
Flyer died

The poetry of life
is never dead
the poetry of life
is not to dread

DAY THREE

At 9 A.M. discussion, the children had many questions for me. Had I brought their hardcover record books? Had I called the Museum of Natural History? For the first time, the children wanted me to answer their questions before they shared everything. They were listening. I told them that I had called the Museum four times but had not gotten through to someone who could help me yet. I promised I would try over and over again today, until I reached someone.

The children didn't have very much to share today, and wanted to get to their work almost immediately. I said I was going to type up the beginning of the story on the primer typewriter, and after that they could begin to arrange it on the pages of a blank book. They left the discussion circle and went to work. The whole class was working so quietly that I asked them if my typing would disturb them. They gave me permission to go ahead.

I typed up the beginning of the story and asked any children who felt like it to join me in the library corner to cut and tape the words into the book. At first four children came over. Very soon, four other boys and girls joined us. The children wanted to examine other books again to see how the sentences were set up. It took us 20 minutes to discuss where to put the first sentence. Finally Meg said, "I'm pooped." I agreed, and she said, "Let's leave it alone right now."

When I went home, I called the Museum of Natural History. An entomologist there agreed to mount Flyer in a plastic container, standing on a twig, just the way he had died. I was relieved that he could be saved and that we could see him again.

As I hung up the phone, I felt a sudden wave of fatigue. I dialed my Aunt Anne's number. I had to talk to someone, and she instinctively understood that to me Flyer's death had not been the passing of a mere butterfly. She was worried about me, and urged me to try to leave it alone for a little while. I assured her that I would try.

DAY FOUR

The children came running into the classroom and practically knocked me over with their excitement. Tyler and Alex had found the first outdoor larvae on an old abandoned road. We wondered together what kind of larvae these might be, and later on the children scoured every book in the classroom to try to find out. I wanted the children to understand that the larvae would need nourishment from their own environment in order to survive in the classroom. The children decided to back-track to the spot where they had found the larvae and look carefully for the leaves that the larvae would need as food. If they could not find them, they would return the larvae to their original place.

I told the children that I had been able to reach the Museum of Natural History, and the Museum's entomologist would mount Flyer. They yelled, "HOORAY!"

The children wanted to work still further on their stories, poetry and pictures about Flyer's life and death. Their enthusiasm seemed endless, and I wondered why. Were they picking up my enthusiasm and my need? But it seemed to be genuinely theirs, too.

While they worked, I started to type my own record of the morning's discussion. They peeked over my shoulder and asked me what I was doing. I said I was keeping my own record book, because they were having so much fun doing theirs. They wanted to see what I wrote.

I showed them that it was what they had said. They grinned when they saw their own words spelled out on paper by their teacher.

Suddenly I felt full of self-doubt. It had started to rain, and the children, perhaps in response to the weather, and perhaps in reaction to me, had started to fight among themselves. They seemed easily upset. I thought I'd better put Flyer's story aside for today. We broke for lunch.

When we came back from lunch it was story time. The children wanted to hear *Goggles* by Ezra Jack Keats. As I read, we examined the layout and pictures once again with our book about Flyer in mind.

After reading time, we continued our group writing on Flyer. When we reached the point in the story when Flyer emerged from his cocoon, James said, "Let's put a poem right there." Remembering the joy of Flyer's birth, we wrote:

> *Our Chrysalis was black*
> *we all thought it was dead*
> *we thought our poor butterfly died*
> *wings emerging*
> *red coming out*
> *left over color from the wing formation*

Meg said, "Could you please type the class poem for us? We can't read script, but we can read your terrible typing." We all laughed, and I went to work with my two-fingered typing.

DAY FIVE

Our morning discussion started at 9 A.M. Adam told about finding a bag containing stolen wallets the night before. One boy, assuming the wallets contained money, asked, "Why didn't you keep it?" Adam answered, "There were special pictures in it and an ID card."

The children who had empathized so readily with Meg when she lost her poetry, were finding compassion for strangers more difficult. I used their feelings about Flyer to help them imagine the feelings of the wallets' owners. I asked, "Which would you want back the most, a picture of Flyer or your money?" They all shouted, "The picture!"

I met with five children who had been having difficulty reading. Although these children could read their own writing, they had resisted reading from the required reader and workbook. This morning I could hardly believe what I heard. Not only were they reading, but they wanted to show off for me. I hugged the whole group—I was so proud!

James had written a play about Flyer, and some of the children read it to each other. I heard one of my former nonreaders reading James' play. Five other children sat in a group making plans for another original play.

After lunch it was story time, and again we examined the book for ideas. Cynthia said, "They used mixed colors." "They were talking to things that weren't alive," said James. "Like the gate, the sky, the cloud, the grass, the fence," Barbara observed. "There was a feeling of spring colors." Meg said, "It makes you feel like you would like to be that person."

The day ended with a happy feeling of pride and accomplishment. We had progressed further on our story about Flyer, and I saw that the children were developing the skills they needed and felt pride in what they had done.

DAY SIX

It was time to start giving the children the Metropolitan Achievement Testing series. I had been worried that the children would react to the testing series as they had reacted to another series of required tests at the beginning of the year. They had been nervous and fidgety, and had bombarded me with questions but seemed unable to hear my directions. I had interpreted their behavior as panic at being tested and judged.

Now, as I started the testing, I was amazed. The children were calm. Their attitude toward the testing routine was, "Well, we've got to do it, so let's get it over with."

After lunch, we had story time, and continued to examine and read a book of their choice. Then we worked further on our class story. Meg said, "You can type a lot of it, but if you want to say something in very big letters, then you can write instead of typing." She also suggested that we keep the book short. "We want the little kids to read our story, and they won't read a long book." We agreed.

Randy asked, "When are we going to get this all together?" In response to his urging, we made a list of the tasks yet to be done. We felt sorry that it was time to clean up and we would have to wait until the next day to start work on our remaining tasks.

Now that the story was finished, I needed to share my feelings about it with other sympathetic adults. I spoke with Sara Miller of the Children's Library at White Plains, and Sara Rubin, a young mime artist who works with children. Sara Rubin suggested re-enacting Flyer's story in movement form. I thought her idea was wonderful and wondered if I could capture the children's movement story in photographs. I went to sleep that night thinking about other ways of telling our story.

DAY SEVEN

During our morning discussion, I told the class that Marion's mother had taken Flyer to New York to be mounted.

Marc asked, "Did you remember that Flyer died standing up?"

"I spoke to the entomologist two nights ago," I said. "He asked me how I would like Flyer mounted, and I told him we wanted him to be standing if possible. He said he would mount him on dry vegetation in a plastic container. He said that Flyer was in a relaxing room in order to separate his legs because they were standing so tightly together."

Marion read her mother's letter to the class.

Dear Mrs. Young's Second Grade Class,

Flyer went to New York City today, to the Museum of Natural History. First Flyer rode in my bike basket to the train station. He jiggled a bit in his box, but he didn't get hurt. Then he rode on the train with a lot of people going to work. The train was not bumpy and he did not get hurt. Then he went through the train station into the subway station. I was glad Flyer was dead, so that he didn't have to smell it. Then he rode the subway uptown to where I work. He sat on top of the file cabinet till lunchtime. Then he went across town on the bus, and at last arrived at the museum. Up the elevator he went, into the office of Entomology. When he is done there, he will be mounted in a glass case.

Do you think if he were alive, he would have liked all that traveling?

Marion's Mom

The children asked to continue working on their Flyer projects before testing. I agreed. When it was time to begin the tests, I hated to stop their work. At the end of the testing session, we decided that we would get to the next day's testing early in the morning so that we wouldn't have to interrupt our work.

After lunch and story time, we had time to work further on Flyer's story. We were all very anxious to write the part of the story when Flyer escaped from his cage and Adam saved his life.

Just as we were going to the playground at the end of the day, Marion said, "I don't know what the title should be, but it should not be mentioning what Flyer is."

DAY EIGHT

Just before we starting testing, I read aloud the whole story of Flyer as we had written it up to that point. Johnny said, "If we could give our Flyer story a score, we'd give him an A+." The whole class seemed to feel an impetus toward finishing the story of Flyer today.

As the day went on, though, I felt a strange sense of nervousness, a feeling that we would never finish our story.

After lunch, we decided to skip story time and begin writing. It was time to write about how Adam saved Flyer's life. As the children wrote Adam's story, Adam felt very special. We remembered that he had done something we all admired and wished we had done. He had followed his impulses and had seemed to know exactly what to do. When he had seen that Flyer was in danger, he had made us all freeze, walked directly to the window, and calmed everybody as he slowly coaxed the trembling Flyer onto his finger and brought him safely back to his cage.

As I listened to the children, I was filled with admiration for Adam.

The class remembered Meg's poetry and wanted to use it to conclude our story.

the poetry of life
is never dead
the poetry of life
is not to dread

Poor Flyer

I thought about the children and our shared experience of Flyer's death. I realized that in expressing our feeling about Flyer's death, we had become more interested, more deeply involved with the activity of our lives. We began to remember the fun we had with Flyer. We became a close-knit family, caring about each other. The children came to love books. Nonreaders began to read. The class became able to face the tension of the testing situation without defending themselves from the pain of performing for judgment. All this had been achieved not through focusing on accomplishment, but through sharing our deepest feelings.

CHAPTER 4

Discovering Interests and Developing the Theme

Trust and caring are not meant to be substitutes, in the classroom, for solid learning. In fact, learning is the point. Trust provides the supportive environment. Feelings that are shared free us up to learn. If the children didn't trust—me, their parents, each other—they wouldn't be willing to go with free-floating interest development. Nor would they be willing, finally, to consolidate into one theme.

It is basic for the children to be able to create, be inventive and produce imaginative solutions in our very complex and ever-changing world. Each child creates in his or her own way as we examine, question and discuss together the problems of sharing in the classroom and the problems in the theme development. We find out how we go about developing a process to learn on our own.

From the first day of school the children are asked to share their interests in a very special way. I have found that merely to ask the children to tell me about their interests is not enough. I ask them first to look about them for things that excite their curiosity. I remind them that there are things at home, things they might pick up in the streets, or from the ponds or pathways. I urge them to bring them to class.

When seven year olds take the time to bring in their collections, the things they have in their rooms at home, things they pick up from the streets, you know there is a strong interest. The next important factor is my response. It is important to the children that what they have shared is of interest to their teacher and their classmates as well. I try to make sure that each child will have clear evidence of my involvement. I take each of the items representing an interest and research it. My research is not profound or complicated. I generally use four key resources: the library, my own resource files, parents and newspapers.

Most of the children's interests are represented in books. My own resource file contains examples and illustrations from previous years of seven-year-old interests. Some vital and dynamic resources are the parents of the children. I routinely survey school files for parent occupation information. Frequently, the children's interests have some relationship to the jobs and professions of their parents.

The subject title catalog in the library is an invaluable resource. Headlines from newspapers periodically offer important connections to the children's interest. I bring books, newspapers and other paraphernalia into the classroom and I use them to share what I found about their interests. I use this opportunity to express my own interest not only in the topic but in the children themselves.

I find some topics are easier to pick up on than others. Technical topics, for example, are often beyond my scope or experience. Nevertheless, I can find something about everything!

Within the first week of school I have usually provided some response to the individually expressed interests of the children. Some teachers may consider this to be an overwhelming first week objective. There is no law that says you must respond to all the children in one week. It actually may take between four and six weeks for them to trust that their interests will be appreciated. Remember that at the same time we are building trust in other ways and practicing problem solving in our daily work and interpersonal relationships.

I have already modeled a theme development when I set up the bulletin boards and room environment so that when the children are looking around for objects of interest, one of the first places I have them look is in the classroom. "I'd like you to explore what we have. Come back and meet with me and we will talk about whether your interest is here or not." Here's the place to see if my pre-planning really covered every child's interest.

What do the questions do? The children see that some questions cannot be answered without more information. Mostly, they see that their questions lead to more questions.

I insist they question everything they do and know that the process is a good one. It allows them to grow and learn.

I don't believe learning is the accumulation of isolated facts. You don't learn something one day and something else the next, with no tie-in. Each area or interest has hundreds of potential relationships to other ideas.

I call these relationships "connections," because I want to demonstrate not just the relationships, but also the continuity and flexibility. I want to illustrate to the children how their interests can broaden and take new and unexpected paths—so that each connection becomes an adventure.

To make connections between the children's interests, we come together for frequent brainstorming sessions. We go back and forth between individual and small group exploration and large group interaction. It is imperative that the children ask questions when they come up and that as a teacher I record those questions. I listen to children's questions and the most important response from me is—"How can we find out more about what you want to know?"

During this one-on-one and small group talking together, I will make a commitment to the children when I feel I can follow up on a trip or an experiment. As a teacher I then find the agency, the person, the books, the trip. Further relationships and connections are made as more questions are asked. In addition, we develop small group projects related to common interests. Eventually, these small group projects will lead to a whole class project, related to the theme.

Brainstorming charts help the children to continue to visualize what they have said. They can see the patterns—the interests that persist and whet their appetites for further exploration.

Eventually, they see the connections in all their random interests, and dabbling turns into education.

Our goal is to discover how each of our individual interests relates to another. We learn that we don't give up anything when we join our interest to someone else's. We only make ours more meaningful. We commit ourselves to search out a common theme and attach our learning to it for a whole year. A whole year keeps our interest alive. We need that time to find resources—make connections—get deeper into the subject. A whole year demonstrates that we can study something our whole lives and never finish. There are always things to be learned and discovered.

When there is a whole year of interest development, no question becomes too silly. There is a sustained dedication to learning. A whole year tells children that as adults they will make a difference. As they become important, so do other things and other people. They listen to other people's points of view. They look at things from many different perspectives. They question. They observe and notice details. They look for the bigger picture. Even a whole year is not enough. What would it be like to pursue learning this way through elementary school?

It doesn't matter how long it takes to identify our common theme. In fact, we can never pinpoint the exact moment when we know what our theme is. There is a point when a theme adopts a label—like insects, or garbage, or fantasy, or city. But actually the theme itself is always evolving and changing, whether it has its label yet or not. I just read through the newsletters of three years of theme development. Each year was different and yet the same.

INSECTS

The children and I explored. They were excited about nature. They liked to talk and share. They could draw magnificently. They hated paper work. They knew they had already failed in reading so they had stomachaches and headaches.

The first day of school, Geoff brought in a hornet's nest. I didn't know it then, but that was the beginning of our theme. In one of our first discussions, Johnny told about squeezing the frog to death—and since frogs aren't important anyway it was all right. That was my clue to develop the hornet's nest into a discussion of nature's balance. I implored Ed Bieber to come over the second week of school with his live bees. The children were enthralled. They sat and listened, observed and asked questions for two hours. What happened to their short attention span?

I raided the White Plains Library with the exuberant help of Sara Miller and brought back all the insect books I could find. I started reading Beatrix Potter to the children. Jeremy Fisher, the frog, became their favorite character. We described the character traits of Beatrix Potter's animals. We began to make up insect characters in our record books. Our record books became a collection of pictures, stories, poetry—a source of pride to each child. I took dictation for the children. A parent came in to help the children record their insect stories.

Meanwhile a number of things were happening. The other second grade was getting piles of paper work. A rap session was started by the other second grade teacher and the first and third grade teachers to discuss "what to do with all these problem children." I found these meetings a terrible source of personal upheaval and frustration. Their concerns about retention and promotion and making sure they could survive with the basics of spelling and reading were coming from a different perspective than mine. They made me question what I was doing. I appeared to be unable to communicate my commitment to a program based on children's interest. It was very uncomfortable even talking about what I do or am trying to do with the children.

I felt alone and unsupported in my endeavors. The only thing that mattered to me was the children—getting them to feel a love of learning and translating that into a love for books and reading.

It was already November. The children and I needed a sense of accomplishment. The class had decided that there were three main veins that they wanted to pursue: make a book, do an insect play and form a society to protect an insect. Clearly our theme had become insects.

We were ready to make an insect book. We had been compiling our own record books for two months. How was I going to get all those lovely pictures out of their books? I decided to xerox as many as I could. I carefully deleted a variety of pictures from each book with the children. Our helpful and understanding secretary, through a very bad cold, made sure that I got the xeroxed pictures by Friday afternoon. She knew I had planned to spend a good part of the weekend trying to find a pattern for arranging the book.

I had previously invited a few parents to come in and record the information that the children had gathered on the specific insects that interested them. We were arranged in groups.

The information poured out and was collected. We published our insect book by December.

When Flyer died, we remembered him together as a class and wrote a special story about his life in our classroom and his death. Together we talked about death in the class. We shared and became a close-knit family.

We examined, compared, classified and made up our own imaginary insects, summarizing and recording everything we learned. As "insect experts," the students knew more than the teacher and became interested in the larger problems of the use of insecticides. They wrote to the Parks Department of Long Island to encourage them not to use Sevin to spray the trees against the gypsy moth caterpillars. They found out about frustration when they were told that once the bureaucracy was in motion, the plan couldn't be stopped. They did not give up, but wrote President Carter about this problem. One of his aides answered us, to no avail, when it came to using Sevin in that park. They tried and tried again and felt they were heard. They will continue to try all their lives.

FANTASY

I had a new group of children. I didn't know anything about them. One little girl was brand new to our school. When we talked about where we were from, she said that her father had a lumber mill. I went over and picked up a number of different samples of wood. There was a beginning. I heard a particular interest. A number of boys seemed to be very interested in sports. So I had wood and sports. I wasn't sure where to go from there, but at least I brought in different samples of wood and labeled them, and we started to compare the wood. Mr. Tandoh from Ghana was in the building. The class made up a list of questions to ask him about the wood from Ghana, and invited him to visit the classroom. He did.

When Mr. Tandoh came in, we became very interested when he told us about a particular tree called the ghost tree. According to belief, the witch doctor can make the tree poisonous if he wishes to kill a person or if that person has been judged by the witch doctor to have done harm in the village. Well, that was the end of wood and the beginning of the discussion of witch doctors. I listened and heard the children extend their curiosity to good-luck vs. bad-luck superstitions. I picked up on their interest in superstitions, but was hesitant to encourage the exploration.

It was important to keep the interest positive, rather than focusing on just the sinister and frightening superstitions. When the children talked about good-luck vs. bad-luck superstitions, they of course focused on the down side: walking under a ladder, seeing a black cat. I sent a note home to parents to ask for superstitions around the world, perhaps that the parents had heard from their own parents. There was a correlation between superstitions and folk tales. One parent, who was a music librarian at SUNY, had a girl in my class who has an adopted Vietnamese sister. He sent us folk tales from Vietnam, which, when I read them to the children, showed a universality of folk tales around the world.

I wanted to find a place to visit that was steeped in legend, that had superstitions. Ed Bieber, who knows and loves the outdoors, took us to Rockland State Park to see the Original Knickerbocker Ice Company and the remains of the original village. There was an old cemetery. The children could reconstruct how the ice was taken from the lake and carried down to the river. It seemed to me we might move from legend to water and water pollution—that type of thing. As a matter of fact, I had Mr. Hooks come in from the water department to tell us about what was happening with our own water in the town and county and in the state. There was a strong interest in this from a few children, but I did not get any overriding excitement from the whole class. The things that kept persisting were the legends and the superstitions. I was looking for some kind of connecting thread. I seemed to have a tree trunk, or a base, of fantasy, legends, monsters of the middle ages, witchcraft. The kids could really relate to these topics. They were mildly curious about the water problems but not with the same enthusiasm as last year's class might have been. That class liked fruit flies and science overall, so that anything that had to do with nature seemed to pervade. This was sort of a branch of the tree but it didn't look like it would take hold with the whole class.

I read to the children every day. The books generally relate to the interest that I am trying to pick up on. Since we were on superstition, moving into fantasy, I was able to get very early in the year into *The Lion, the Witch and the Wardrobe*, by C.S. Lewis. The children absolutely loved it. A short time after I had finished the book, there was an article in the *New York Times* that said that the play would be produced on TV. The children said, "It's going to take them two years. It could take us two months—Let's do it." Their enthusiasm for the story told me that was the route that I could put most of my energies into. All of the children in some way could participate.

I didn't immediately connect the theme to our writing, but one little boy had created a fantasy character, and it became easy to develop characters such as Pen and Pencil, Woolly and Bear, Paint and Brush and Every and Thing. The children and their enthusiasm dictate the type of language arts experiences we have in the classroom. The children who, in another year, loved Haiku poetry, transferred their interest to other types of poetry and literature. This year's class enjoyed fanciful reading and writing. I hope they will love books and will read to their children some day.

GARBAGE

I first saw a fruit beginning to rot and attract the fruit flies. My first inclination was to throw it out, because the custodians would complain and because it smelled bad. But I said, "NO, the children are attracted to the smell and to the fruit flies." I thought, "Let's cover it up and see what happens."

The important thing is not that I left the rotting fruit there, but that I saw that the children were attracted to it. Then I had to find and bring in items that were related, such as articles about the garbage problem. I took the children to the Sanitary Landfill. We invited experts to talk about the problems of garbage and the use of energy. We brought in books and we related our writing and reading experiences to fruit flies and genetics. The children who were most interested in fruit flies visited SUNY and we began to get into the whole genetics area. The total environmental experience was involved.

Thus, not only did I have to sense that the interest had potential, I had to see if the children picked up on it. When I saw that they did, then I could introduce other information and experiences that would let them get in touch with the bigger problem. It was important to see if I could get the whole class in some way involved.

It doesn't really matter what we are studying about, whether it is fruit flies or fantasy. Actually not knowing is part of the excitement for me as a teacher. The most important questions are not the ones that I have, but the ones that the children have. It is because of the questions that the children will begin to read and learn about the things that they are interested in.

CITY

This year I looked closely at the theme development. I thought at first Barry's strong interest in dinosaurs would be contagious. It did not spread. The ideas that take hold are the themes that you can put your hands on.

September 10, 19—

Dear Parents,

Children are willing to learn more about the things and events that interest them personally. Much of my work—especially at the beginning of the year—is to listen for clues to those interests. Sometimes the children don't know what those interests are or if they are important. So we have the exciting task of finding out together.

My job is to present the possibilities through guest speakers and visitors, going on trips, reading books, magazines and newspapers as well as contacting governmental and community groups. During this process I listen to hear what is clicking and will continue to hold their interest. Once we have developed a focus, we begin to make connections—that involves the entire "finding out process" of listening, summarizing, reporting, recording and sharing themselves as well as the information.

I asked the children to bring anything that interested them into the classroom during the first week of school. Based on what I heard and saw, I did some simple research and selected some books that they could read themselves and others for me to read aloud. Ask your child to tell you about those books. Help me listen to where those interests lie. Your participation will make a difference!

Books are an integral part of this finding out process. I want children to become readers who not only learn to read but read to learn—and enjoy it. That enjoyment can be fostered and encouraged by me and by you. Let's discuss that as well as what I hope to accomplish this year. I have arranged an evening at the White Plains Public Library with Sara Miller, Children's Services Director. Sara is a former member of the Newberry Award Committee and currently on the American Library Association's Notable Children's Books Committee. More importantly, she is an enthusiastic collaborator in this process we are discussing. We work together throughout the year and I want you to meet her, hear about reading and books and see how you can make use of the resources she has available for you.

PLEASE COME ON THURSDAY EVENING, SEPTEMBER 20th FROM 7:30 TO 9:00 P.M.

Come with questions. This is going to be quite a year.

Sincerely,
Elaine Young

The maps I had placed around the room in my pre-planning led the children to speculate about roads, which led me to invite Stephanie's father to discuss the Hutchinson River Parkway.

September 12, 19—

Dear Parents,

Stephanie's father will visit our classroom on Monday, September 17th at 9:30 A.M. We made some assumptions about his job as Supervisor for the Department of Transportation, working on the Hutchinson River Parkway. We assume he is the Boss of Making Roads.

1) Jay assumes he wears a hat with a light in the middle.

2) Randy assumes he wears working shoes.

3) Jeremy assumes that if someone is not working he talks to them.

4) Natalie assumes he just sits there and watches to make sure if they're doing it right.

5) Caitlin assumes he helps his workers sometimes.

6) Matthew assumes he tells the workmen what to do.

7) Mrs. Young assumes he knows how to read maps.

Questions for Stephanie's Father

1) Jay: Did he need a degree before he worked on the roads?

2) Janine: What kinds of tools does he need to work with?

3) Randy: What kind of wood does he work with?

4) Caitlin: Is it easy or hard working on the roads?

5) Karie: How do they start digging the dirt?

6) Ryan: How do they pave it and fix it?

7) Mrs. Young: How do they choose where to put the road?

8) Coby: How do they make white and yellow lines?

9) Barry: How much time does it take to work on a road and finish it?

10) Jeremy: Does stuff fall on your head?

11) Natalie: If there are two roads to be fixed, how do they choose which one to do first?

12) Fred: What do they put under the gravel?

We feel good that Stephanie's father is coming in and we want to know a lot about roads.

From Mrs. Young's Second Grade

P.S. Please join us if you can. Do you have any questions?

The trips and visitors either firm up an interest or show a lead to be false. The books Sara sent from the library on bridges, dams, barges and canals sparked a real interest. Groups of children made large murals depicting each.

Ryan's grandfather lives on the other side of the Brooklyn Bridge, so Ryan made a picture of it. Barry loved the dam book and told Ryan there were dams built under the Brooklyn Bridge to keep the water aside. Jay, Jeremy and Fred loved barges and drew the largest one they could, carrying everything they could think of from cars to sand to wheat.

A trip to the construction site across the street showed a bridge and a dam, right there, where they're building a tunnel through a stream, whetting the appetites of the children and myself for narrowing down the connections. Pat Angarano, the Town Supervisor, came in and clearly defined the Hutchinson River Parkway problem in Harrison. He showed us where three lanes merge into two, resulting in congestion of traffic, air pollution—and angry people. We were interested in the talking battle the people were having to get the road fixed.

At this point I could see us looking at the whole state, rebuilding the roads and bridges. Or I could see us studying the more specific problem of designing roads, with three lanes going into two, and all of the ramifications involved. We made a road brainstorming chart.

BRAINSTORMING MAP ABOUT ROADS

TRAILS
Animal Trails
Nature Trails
Foot Trails
Computer Trails
Motorcycle Trails

WATERWAYS
Hudson River — bridges
Croton River — dam
Canals — ferry
airways
train tracks

ROADS
One chop–two chop
Three chop roads
Corduroy roads
Pebble roads
Oyster Shell Roads
mail — Old Post Road
Dirt Bike Roads

Ways to find out more about Trails and Roads

Books—Magazines—Maps—Trips—Visitors
Studying Maps   Making Scale Models
Writing Letters   Making a Magazine with
Asking Questions   our Information

The children were also talking about making a kid's show on radio, or designing a magazine or building a model of a bridge and dam and road inside or outside.

I was at a twofold point. I kept feeding into the stated and implied interest with trips and visitors and still listened for new interests and enthusiasms. We planned to take a trip to a bridge and a dam. I looked for an engineer. I brought in the people who were having the talking battle. I contacted a judge to talk about what happens when people sue each other.

December 7, 19—

Matthew and Janine
Mrs. Young's Second Grade Class
Purchase Elementary School
Purchase, New York

Dear Matthew and Janine:

Supervisor Pat Angarano has sent me a copy of your letters about the Hutchinson River Parkway. I am very pleased to learn that you also are concerned about what is being done to our local parkway.

Although I am a surgeon by profession, I am also a citizen. That means I must be concerned about problems which affect my neighborhood and my town. I have formed the CONCERNED CITIZENS FOR A SAFER HUTCH, along with a group of Westchester homeowners and business people, to ask for changes in the plan for rebuilding the Hutchinson River Parkway. There are many things that we feel are wrong with the present plan.

It would be a pleasure to speak to your class and to tell you what may happen to the parkway, if we cannot change it. Please ask Mrs. Young to call me at my office if you would like me to speak to you and to answer your questions.

Yours sincerely,
Peter S. Liebert, M.D.

State of New York
EXECUTIVE CHAMBER
Albany 12224
Mario M. Cuomo
Governor

November 19, 19—

Dear Boys and Girls:

I want to thank you very much for the invitation to visit your class and answer questions that you have regarding government and, in particular, questions about the building of our roads.

I regret that my schedule is such that I am unable to be with you, but I want to express to you how proud I am of all of you that are interested in government so much that you would like to meet with government officials. I hope that you will carry this interest with you throughout all of your lives and that many of you will choose careers in government, because it is only with such good people as yourselves serving in government that we can have a good and efficient government.

Please continue to do the good work that you are doing and don't ever lose your interest in being of service to others.

Sincerely,
Mario M. Cuomo

Brainstorming identifies the specific areas of interest to be followed—what trips?—what visitors?—what letters?—what people? Our speakers help us to make new connections among our interests and get closer to a theme. The connections help guide the information into a coherent learning pattern with goals and directions.

Sometimes parents are concerned that our work looks like too much fun. They say "Are you doing roads all day long? Sometimes you can't like the things you're learning—life's not like that." Their concerns should not be ignored. I regularly discuss with the children and their parents what has been accomplished. We summarize what we've learned, using their stories, their plays, their poems, their drawings and their paintings, as well as their workbooks and other paper/pencil assignments.

The "fun" that the children refer to, however, is not mere amusement or enjoyment sometimes associated with play, games or sports. It is the excitement that accompanies the discovery that they can find out things that lead to new questions and new potential discoveries. It is this association that keeps the interest high, keeps the interest in classroom activity high, keeps the interest in writing and reading high, keeps the interest in research high and keeps the interest in learning high.

It is not always easy for me to allay the fears of anxious parents. This year we took longer than usual to develop the theme. When it was not immediately apparent how and when the skills were being taught, a group of parents requested that I teach the skills to all of the children at the same time in a sequence they could follow. I wanted to accommodate their need without letting go of our quest for a theme, so I developed some sequential teacher-directed lessons and then attempted tying them to our interests.

I found it easy and yet hard to teach in teacher-directed lessons. The time required to prepare a whole-class math lesson about area and volume is actually less than I would spend making it possible for the children to learn area and volume in the context of the theme, but I seem to become more exhausted because I'm working against my own instincts. There is a real infusion of energy for me and the children in the free-flowing interaction and exchange of ideas and interests. We seem to learn more, and more quickly, than we do with single disconnected lessons.

By trying too hard to respond, I took time away from the connections between interest and learning. The students began to seek "100's" rather than new ideas that would move the theme forward. In particular, Karie and Caitlin, who like to be best and get everything perfect, went from participation and involvement to "I'm not interested in roads anymore. I don't know what I'm interested in." Their comments had a negative effect on some of the children and their motivation. "We don't want to read that story aloud to you. We already read it to ourselves and it's boring to do it again." After the first poetry publication, "We're not so proud of it; we don't like our covers" and concerning the use of the math work book, "We don't want to work in the red math book; we already know it." As a result, I felt the children were not willing to make the commitment that I ask of them in their learning.

With the holidays coming, I put aside our quest for a theme. I put the class back into the more traditional mode of paper and pencil work and furthered other areas of interest that I wanted to develop this year.

We had become very involved with poetry, and I read aloud books that the children loved. I arranged for the children to share their poetry and read aloud on the radio. We also made a commitment to writing a script for our own production of Alan Arkin's *The Lemming Condition*. Holidays, bulletin boards and concerts supplemented our work and filled the time. I sent a newsletter home to let the parents know where we were and invited them to be more aware of interests in the everyday lives of their children. This enabled all of us to step back, take a break and recover our enthusiasm.

December 7, 19—

Elaine Young
Purchase School

Dear Parents:

It's so good to feel well again after such a long battle with the flu! So many of us were affected. We've had to sit down and go over all our earlier ideas and plans. Our theme is fascinating, though not entirely linked.

With the holidays so near, we're taking some "settling in" time now for exploration and consideration. We've made an "Interest Tree" together which will show you what we've developed so far.

Some projects have already been suggested by the class:

1) Construct a model of the Brooklyn Bridge.

2) Make a model of the Hutchinson River Parkway problem in Harrison.

3) Make a dam.

4) Make a city with everything mentioned on the Interest Tree. That city would show now or long ago or even in the future.

We haven't decided exactly how to go about doing these projects, but I have some thoughts about ways to make them seem more concrete.

1) Locate a city planner.

2) Visit a bridge or a dam.

3) Have the people battling over the Hutch come in and debate the issue in the classroom.

4) Persuade the governor or a colleague to visit and talk about roads.

Between now and the New Year, please take time to observe the world around you and see how bridges and roads and dams and tunnels connect with your own lives and interests. Talk to your kids. We're still entirely open to new ideas about projects and how to do them.

Meanwhile, our love of Jumanji and Shel Silverstein's poetry is leading us to the WFAS radio station next week for a tour and taping session. And we have begun writing a script for our own production of Alan Arkin's *The Lemming Condition*.

(That's a major project too and will be some time in the making!)

In January we'll match enthusiasm to project and get going on our main theme. I'll let you know more about the specific skills used and extended by these projects when we're underway.

Happy Holidays.

Best Wishes,
Elaine Young

I came back to school after the Christmas vacation with a renewed enthusiasm and energy. I asked the children what projects and plans they still wanted to pursue. There was a immediate and strong affirmation—Ryan wanted to build the Brooklyn Bridge with Matthew and Jay. They also said I had promised they could build a replica of the Hutch congestion problem.

The roads and bridges just naturally led the children into talking about a whole city. They had been making buildings in the math corner with the rods, volume cubes and pattern blocks. They brought in model cars and airplanes and began naming the buildings they were making. I recalled that at the beginning of the year they liked making buildings right away. Randy insisted we make the city. Barry was adamant about including the dam. Karie and Caitlin did not want to be left out and said they would do all of the other stuff we needed like people, lights, signs and rocks. Stephanie, Natalie and Esther wanted to be responsible for all the stores. Matthew and Coby wanted to make sure we would not leave out tunnels. Jeremy was still saying he wanted be the tour guide for the city and telling us not to forget the train station because he had one in his basement.

The fact that the city was shaping up to be many different kinds of houses and from different parts of the world demonstrated the group dynamics in the class. There were many leaders who wanted to do things their own way. A certain cohesiveness that had been present in most other years was not there. I hoped the play would have a big impact on their team spirit and that the city would be completed with the children having learned social studies, math, reading and writing skills, as well as the skill of cooperating.

I saw individuals who wanted to start on separate projects and my challenge would be to get them together so they could see that what they were doing was really working as a team. They would need to help and support each other. The process of gathering information and planning would be a cooperative effort.

Once again, I did my own brainstorming about how I might help the interests expand and come together. I discarded in my mind those projects that had proven to be deadends, and pondered upon the ideas that were both recurring and "doable."

Could we really build a city and connect the interests of everyone? What city? A real one or an imaginary one? How could we include all of the information we gathered from our trips, visitors and books? Did I want most of the work done in school? How could I get parents involved without their taking over from the children? I was anxious to have the parents see that young children can learn to think and take responsibility for their own learning.

The play took place in March. It was a fantastic success. Students, parents and faculty were exuberant in their praise. But the most extraordinary benefit was for us as a class, because we could see what we had accomplished as a group.

Shortly after that, we decided to build a city in miniature. Karie and Caitlin had become so involved in the play that they really wanted to share. They were the first ones to say "How come we haven't built the city yet?" I told them they would have to learn about electricity and drawing to scale—two topics that just happened to be in our curriculum.

Meanwhile, the children were all reading like crazy and exploring solutions to math problems related to construction and design. Every single one had grown intellectually by every observable and measurable standard. It happens every year as if by magic, but still I'm never sure it will. Every year I wonder whether this will be the year the class doesn't come together—when learning will be random and sporadic or dull and routine. Maybe the wondering is part of the excitement of discovery. It is certainly true that each year I feel the same joy at their awakening as I felt in my first year of teaching.

CHAPTER 5

Tying Together the Thinking Skills

Teaching from a child's interests means that I nurture the child's sensitivity to the world around him. For a child to grow, he has to know what he sees, be able to describe what he sees and be able to draw conclusions from what he sees. I consciously develop within the child specific ways of observing and analyzing his life experiences. These ways are often referred to as the thinking skills. Some consider them to be merely logic. Others would describe them as creative or artistic. The thinking I propose for the children is intuitive, reflective and responsive. It is both logical and creative.

Problem solving is the point. It doesn't matter whether the problem to be solved involves sharing, personal decision-making or a major crisis. It doesn't matter whether the problem is large or small, individual or group related, ethical or social. The process is the same. The thinking skills cooperate to solve the problem.

In order to solve a problem, we have to hypothesize or make some assumptions about the problem. When we make assumptions, we call upon the thinking skills of observing, comparing, classifying or arranging and summarizing.

Observing is a way of gathering information. It is seeing, hearing, smelling, touching, noticing, finding. It is the process of seeing as important the smallest detail. Children are particularly good at observing. They readily hear a bird's song, smell the clean air. They can't always put together what they have observed in a meaningful way, however. They need to develop new skills.

Comparing takes observing a step further. The children practice noticing differences and similarities between things or thoughts they have observed. In the classroom, we compare color, size, texture, odor, taste and mood. We begin by comparing objects and grow into comparing ideas and opinions.

Among the things in the science corner are shells, rocks and bones placed for the purpose of enabling the children to observe, compare, rearrange and place in categories. I use these words from the first day of school. The signs I place near the materials ask children to observe and compare the shells, observe and compare the rocks, observe and compare the bones, observe and compare all of the things on the table. I ask, "How are these things alike and different?" I take time to list the things they say and place them on large charts. This is the beginning of reading the things we have said; seeing our own words. We then define in our own words what we mean by "Observe," "Compare" and "Arrange."

Sept. 21, 19—

Dear Parents,

Class 2Y would like to keep you informed about our progress with our naturalist visitor, Ed Bieber. Our first afternoon together was a stimulating exploring time for Ed, Elaine, the children and visitors Mrs. C and Mrs. W. We began with a discussion that explored our interests. The major areas of interest were animals, reptiles and animal homes. Questions arose about what to do when we bring animals into the room.

How long should they stay?
What should they eat?
When should we touch them?

How can we tell their age?

Are stories we have heard about these animals true or not?

We decided to take a nature walk to look for clues to animal homes on the Manhattanville grounds. We discovered many clues.

Clue #1: Some holes we found may be entrances or exits to animal homes.

Clue #2: A chipmunk or squirrel may have had a breakfast of hickory nuts. We found nuts eaten on the path in several places.

Clue #3: Slugs were living on the underside of a piece of wood. Perhaps it was because of the dampness.

Jerry found a caterpillar. It will be making a cocoon shortly and will spend the winter there. In the spring, it will emerge as a moth or a butterfly. We will make a home for it. We have to think of experiments to find out what it will eat.

Josh found an insect that looks like a spider, but a spider has eight legs. This insect has six legs.

Jon found a grasshopper and we will make a home for it. We have to experiment to see what foods it will eat. We are trying different kinds of leaves.

We discovered many clues about leaves. We saw poison ivy. We recognized it by its three leaves. Sometimes it crawls like a vine. Sometimes it grows on the ground. Sometimes it is like a small bush. Another leaf next to the poison ivy had more leaves on its stem. It had "itches" on it. Poison ivy leaf is all smooth and has no teeth. Poison ivy has berries. Ed told us that 89 kinds of birds eat these berries. There is some good and not all bad in things.

We discovered clues to seed homes. The bean sack was used as an Indian rattle. Indians made things from nature. Seeds rattled and made music. Another seed house was squeezed. The heat from our hands made it explode. The plant from this seed has another Indian legend. The Indians called it jewel weed. They thought it was magic. It grows by the water. If you put the green leaf in the water, it is a silver color. Underwater, it looks like aluminum foil.

Therefore, they thought it looked like a jewel.

Many children found rocks with quartz and with mica. Sand on the beach is made up of tiny pieces of quartz like the one we found. Mica peels off like glass. The pioneers used large pieces of mica as windows.

We observed an old abandoned church on the grounds. The home of a spider web was found by the front door. Webs are all different. Perhaps we will study them. We found a mud wasp's nest. It is made of mud and is a nursery for wasps.

We stopped by a spruce tree. We found dried sap. It was like a scab over the wound of the tree where it was injured. We cut off a wad of dried sap. The Indians used to chew it for gum. The Indians did something to the sap before chewing it. We will try to find out. "If in doubt, don't put anything in your mouth!"

A large hole by the path caught our attention. We were not sure it was an animal home. Maybe a tree trunk came out and an animal used it later as a home.

An animal was sighted. "How to Observe" is important for our future experiences.

After the trip, Ed and Elaine reviewed our first session. We anticipate the following areas of interest to be carried through in the classroom until next Thursday.

1. Make a science corner.
2. Collect books about our interests: caterpillars, grasshoppers, seeds and rocks.
3. Make homes for the caterpillar and the grasshopper.
4. Focus on various types of thinking opportunities.
5. Observe—what Ed wore, the characteristics of the insect we have.
6. Compare—the grasshopper with the caterpillar; poison ivy with other leaves; quartz rocks with mica rocks.
7. Read folk tales aloud, to discover old uses for our treasures.

Elaine and Ed will talk further during the week and plan for next Thursday afternoon. At present, we plan some seed experiments. We are planning and coordinating our trip to Hook Mountain for the hawk watch.

DO YOU SEE YOURSELF AS A RESOURCE PERSON TO ADD TO OUR INFORMATION? PLEASE LET US KNOW IF YOU CAN CONTRIBUTE BOOKS, MAGAZINES, PICTURES, IDEAS OR YOURSELVES.

TRY TO VISIT WITH US ONE THURSDAY AFTERNOON FROM 1 TO 3 FOR SCIENCE TIME.

Mrs. Young's Second Grade Class

I let the children know right away what they are doing. I use the thinking terms in all of our activities. When I ask children to compare characters in a story, they have already internalized the process. I have begun teaching and using the thinking skills.

Classifying, or arranging, is a way of sorting out what we have compared. When we classify, we put things or ideas into categories. For example, if, by observing and comparing, we see a group of creatures with four legs and fur, we can classify them as mammals. We start out by classifying things in the classroom, calling tables and chairs furniture. We move to classifying points of view.

Ed Bieber and I wanted to help the children observe, compare and classify parts of nature as they exist during the winter. We decided that looking for various types of winter homes would give the children that experience. When we returned from our trip, I asked the children to tell me what they saw. They reported their observations in random, disconnected fashion. I asked them if they saw things that were either alike or different. For our comparing exercise, the children used similes which had been introduced earlier in language exercises; e.g., as big as, as hard as, as hot as, etc. The children were asked to compare physical features of the objects observed.

By finding similarities in unlike objects, the children discovered that things are much more alike than they are different. The following newsletter illustrates the classification chart we developed from our comparisons. We classified our findings by their physical features and by the process we used to discover them.

Dec. 12, 19—

Dear Parents,

Yesterday, we took a walk and discovered winter homes with Ed. Here is our classification chart.

	Classification by feature		Classification by process	
Name	**Size**	**Color**	**Where**	**How**
larvae	as big as a queen ant	white	in a home	cutting open the gall
insects	a little smaller than your pencil eraser	blue brown rust red	under the grass and dirt	digging
ground-hog	smaller than size of hole	didn't see	in the field	accident
stream	long, skinny	clear water, muddy bottom	through the field	walking listening smelling seeing

Mrs. Young's Second Grade Class

Summarizing is a hard skill for the children to master. Observing details is more fun and comes more naturally to them. Summarizing requires the opposite ability—to see the big picture, the main idea, the whole point. The children in the classroom learn to sift, skim, condense and throw away what doesn't belong. Summarizing is a necessary final step in making assumptions, or assuming.

Once our observing, comparing, classifying and summarizing have led to the development of some assumptions, we come to the next major problem-solving function. We have to test our hypothesis, or see if our assumptions are accurate. Since children are not researchers, their ways of testing are more imaginative than scientific, but they still use the basic thinking skills required of more experienced problem solvers. They need to gather data, review alternatives, state and defend positions and imagine or invent solutions.

Gathering or collecting data can be more interesting for children than it might seem. As the following newsletter will demonstrate, gathering data can mean investigating the habits of caterpillars, grasshoppers and fruit flies. It can also mean working within the curriculum and learning to find answers from books.

We had a winter problem. The fruit flies we had been breeding died. Some of the children believed that it was because of the cold. Others believed it was because the food was used up. The children assumed that if the insects died because of the cold or because the food supply was used up, then they should live with warmth and food. They decided to test their assumption about the cold first. They used four food jars and created four environments that were exactly the same except that they wanted to raise the temperature. Here is the newsletter that describes the experiment.

Jan. 23, 19—

Dear Parents,

Do you remember when we found a caterpillar and it made a cocoon in our classroom? Now after about three months, it has come out from its pupa stage. It looks like a dead bumble bee. It is black. The cocoon was light brown. We are waiting for the moth or butterfly to spread its wings. We think it happened before spring because our room was a lot hotter than outdoors.

Do you remember when we brought the insect home, called a gall, into our classroom? Well, the larva which was inside the gall turned into a wasp, but the container was closed so it died. It couldn't get air. So far, the insects we have, the caterpillar, the wasp and the fruit fly, have larva and pupa stages.

John wants to know if the grasshopper has a larva and pupa stage also. We are investigating.

Next Tuesday, Feb. 8, two fifth grade boys from an elementary school in Irvington will visit our classroom to learn about our fruit flies and insects. Mrs. Williams, a special teacher in that district, will bring the boys at 9:30 A.M.

OUR FRUIT FLIES HAVE DIED.

WE THINK IT IS BECAUSE OF THE COLD.

We will do an experiment to see if it is the cold. We have four baby food jars. We want to have the same amount of sunlight. We want to have the same amount of moisture. We want to have the same amount of food. We want to have the same amount of pupa.

Our problem is how to change the temperature. That is the only thing we want to change. Gene, Kyle, Dean, Ricky, Scott and Mike made the following suggestions which we will try.

One jar will have a mirror behind it to reflect the sunlight. We assume that will make it hotter.

One jar will have a piece of paper with holes in it for the sunlight to seep through.

One jar will have plastic wrap around it. We assume that will make it warmer.

One jar will have clay around it. We assume it won't reflect the sun and heat.

We will keep you informed about what happens.

Mrs. Young's Second Grade Class

The reader should know that even though there was plenty of food, and even though the temperature in the jars was 25 degrees centigrade, just the right temperature for fruit flies, THE FRUIT FLIES DIED.

We had assumed that the fruit flies died because of the cold. We gathered data by conducting an experiment with the four jars, and we are still in the dark about why the fruit flies died. We planned on ordering more fruit flies, but what could we have done in the meantime to test our assumptions? We could review the alternatives and state and defend our positions.

Reviewing alternatives causes the children to choose between one possible answer and another. In the process of making the choice, children are free to weigh the information and still come up with different conclusions.

Stating and defending positions is exciting for children who have learned to trust themselves and each other in the classroom. When no opinion is regarded as stupid, children love to express their views. Confusing information or prejudice may cause children to have different ideas of the truth. Stating and defending a position helps everyone to separate fact from opinion.

While there is no newsletter describing the process with fruit flies as the topic, the following newsletter illustrates the way in which members of another class express themselves on a different topic—the existence of the Loch Ness Monster.

Dear Parents,

We have been reading about the Loch Ness monster, and we have made some assumptions about whether he exists or not. In order to test our assumptions, we are stating and defending our positions based on what we have read, seen on television and heard from parents and other adults.

Paul: I believe in Nessie because if people put the photographs in the book, I believe it, because how could it be a trick. An artist can't do that.

Michael: I'm half and half. I'm not sure it's alive or not. I know that they use trick photography. They do it in television and things can be taken out and put into photographs.

Laura: So many people tell me what I should think. If I'm not really sure, I need more information. I think we should wait until someone catches it or gets a very clear picture.

Liz: I believe in Nessie because we studied about him and we've done a lot of things about him, and I think that he's alive.

Florence: I believe in Loch Ness because if there wasn't a Loch Ness Monster, they wouldn't be talking about him.

Bonny: I believe in Loch Ness because on TV they showed the same photographs as in the book.

Mrs. Young's Second Grade Class

Imagining or inventing allows children to come up with extraordinary solutions. In the process of brainstorming, they can let go of what is real or practical and make believe anything is possible. Later, they sort out the workable aspects of what they have imagined and apply them to the real problem at hand.

On an entirely different theme, the following newsletter offers samples of Haiku poetry written by the children. Haiku presents children with the opportunity to see an image in a tight, brief, concise form. It is made up of only three lines, the first containing five syllables, the second containing seven syllables and the third reverting to five syllables. Haiku usually deals with nature in its most fundamental sense. The image must, in a few words, capture a universal meaning.

I use Haiku to encourage children to see nature and themselves in common terms. I ask them to imagine that they are a raindrop, or a tree, or the wind, or the rocks or the chair. In the following exercise, I have asked the children to become things in the room. Ordinary objects are given life through the children's imagination, and they can never be ordinary again. Imagining in this way trains children to use imagination in problem solving and teaches them that imaginary solutions can be useful in developing real life answers to real life problems. There is a connection between fantasy and fact.

March 3, 19—

Dear Parents,

We want to share our Haiku poetry with you.

THINGS IN OUR ROOM
*AM A BLADE OF GRASS * I AM A BLADE OF GRASS TOO
* AM A BLADE OF GRASS *

*I AM SOMEONE'S LUNCH * PEOPLE EAT ME UP AND
QUICK * I DO NOT LIKE IT *

*I AM A MATH BOOK * I'M HARD SOMETIMES I'M EASY
* I'M FINISHED NOW *

*LIKE TO BE SAT IN * PEOPLE LIKE TO SIT IN ME GOOD
* LOVE TO BE SAT IN *

*AM SAD ABOUT YOU * FEEL BAD AND YOU SAT ON ME
* SOMEONE SAT ON ME *

*NICE CLOCK YES TICK TOCK * IT'S NICE TO BE TICK-
ING YES * CLOCK TICK TOCK TICK TOCK *

*NICE TO BE A CLOCK * EVERYTIME PEOPLE LOOK AT ME
* TICK TOCK TICK TOCK CLOCK *

*CHAIR FEELS LIKE WOOD DOLL * THE RODS FEEL LIKE A BARE TREE * TABLE HAS FOUR LEGS **

*AM A FUNNY BOOK * YOU SAY I AM A BOOK OH * I LIKE YOU GOOD BOOK **

*I'M A ROCK FROM GROUND * I'M A BIG ROCK FROM THE GROUND * A GOOD ROCK FROM GROUND **

*I AM A ROD NOW * I AM BEING BUILT WITH NOW * I AM STILL A ROD **

*I AM A ROUND GOURD * I CAN ROLL AROUND PLACES * I DROPPED OH NO BYE **

*I AM A WHITE ROD * LIKE TO BE LITTLE WHITE ROD * AM A SMALL ROD TOO **

*I AM A BIG BOOK * PEOPLE READ ME EVERY DAY * I FEEL VERY LIKED **

*I AM A WARM CHAIR * WHO IS COLD CHAIR I AM * WHO IS NICE CHAIR **

*I AM A BIG CHAIR * PEOPLE SIT ON ME A LOT * I LIKE TO BE HERE **

*I AM TOOTSIE WHEN * I AM FRIGHTENED VERY MUCH * SOMETIMES THEY HOLD ME **

*PEOPLE SIT ON ME * I AM WOOD AND STEEL HARD STEEL * I'M HARD WOOD VERY **

*I AM A PIECE OF GRASS * I GROW VERY VERY TALL * I'M A TOMATO **

*TICK TOCK GOES THE CLOCK * TICK TOCK TICK TOCK TICK TOCK TICK * THE CLOCK GOES TICK TOCK **

Mrs. Young's Second Grade Class

Moving back and forth between fantasy and the real world to solve a problem is a real challenge. Once a hypothesis or assumption has been tested and argued, and answers and solutions have been imagined, the children need to come to a conclusion or a consensus. Usually, the consensus leads to a course of action, which in turn leads to new problems to solve, and the process begins again. Each new problem means the steady and methodical application of the thinking skills.

We use the thinking skills consciously. It is not enough for us, as a class, to let thinking skills creep into what we are doing in random fashion. If children don't know what, how and when they're thinking, they can't use the skills whenever they want to, in ways to fit the circumstances. The child who is aware of his own thinking and problem-solving process has a better chance of calling those skills into play whenever he needs them.

The following letters illustrate how we, as a class, solved a real world problem, using the thinking skills, and how we became involved in an issue of concern to our parents and friends in the county.

One day, I was reading an article to the children expressing concern over garbage disposal and solid waste management. At about the same time, we received a crate of oranges for an outdoor cooking experience. When we opened the orange crate we found that a few of the oranges had molds on them. When we touched the mold, we observed tiny spores or seeds. In a class experiment, the children observed that oranges could be "eaten up" by the molds. If the molds could "eat up" garbage, this might be a possible solution to the county garbage problem. It was time to test their hypothesis.

Hon. Alfred DelBello
County Executive
County Office Building
White Plains, New York

Dear Mr. DelBello,

We read your newspaper article about the garbage. We would like to help clean up the county. We have been studying about molds, and we are wondering if molds could help you.

We have molds in our classroom. We could send you one of our molds to put near the garbage to show you how it eats up the garbage. Would you describe what you are doing right now with the garbage? We want to help you.

1. If the molds make the garbage into dirt, what do you do with the dirt?

2. How do you get any bad germs out of the dirt?
3. Where do you put the garbage now?
4. Can you make some of the paper into newspaper?
5. Could you use molds to destroy the garbage?
6. Do you send garbage to farms for pigs to eat?
7. Could you build something to hold the garbage so the molds could eat it little by little?
8. Could the wine bottles be cut in half and used for glasses?

Please write us or call us or visit our class to tell us how we can help.

Sincerely,

Mrs. Young's Second Grade Class

The children made some observations about the effect of the mold on the oranges. They classified oranges as potential garbage and hypothesized that if the mold works on the oranges, surely it will work on the garbage. Their assumptions led them to think about the garbage problem and to come up with other possible solutions.

I want to keep them thinking and keep their interest alive. By immediately writing down their questions and assumptions in the form of a letter to the county executive, I have told them their ideas are important and given them an opportunity to test them out. It is not always easy for me to type up their questions exactly as they come out. Sometimes I think, "Can't you think of a better question?" I have to tell myself that what they ask is what they want to know.

The following letters from Mr. DelBello and Gerald Clarke show the children that real and responsible people are taking them seriously as problem solvers. The solid waste problem becomes something they can sink their teeth into. They can do anything.

Dear Mrs. Young,

Thank you for directing your class's attention to a matter of such community concern as is our Solid Waste Management Program.

I read the class's letter and questions with interest and, as you know, have already asked Gerald Clarke of the Department of Solid Waste Management to work with you in formulating answers.

I do appreciate you generating such civic enthusiasm in your second graders and the opportunity to be of assistance.

Enclosed is a letter to the class, preliminary to Mr. Clarke's more detailed reply. Thank you again for writing.

Sincerely,
Alfred B. DelBello
County Executive

Dear Mrs. Young,

I am enclosing a letter to your class which I hope will answer some of the questions which were asked concerning how garbage is handled in Westchester County and what our current problem is.

The project your class did with the molds is similar to composting, where bacteria convert organic material to a mixture that looks like dirt and can be used as a soil conditioner.

Our problem in Westchester County is that we have so much solid waste, 900,000 tons a year, that if we were to compost it, we would still have an awful lot of compost to get rid of, which is exactly the problem raised in question #1: If the molds make the garbage into dirt, what do you do with the dirt?

Let me try and answer the rest of your questions.

1. How do you get any bad germs out of the dirt? The high temperatures reached in the composting process kill the bad germs.

2. Where do you put the garbage now? The garbage is now burned in municipal and apartment incinerators or goes to a landfill.

3. Can you make some of the papers into newspaper? Only if you separate the newspapers first. When paper is mixed with other garbage, it gets too dirty and then it costs too much to try and clean it for reuse.

4. Could you use molds to destroy the garbage? Yes, but they take too long to eat it and much much longer to eat the cans, and they won't eat bottles.

5. Do you send garbage to farms for pigs to eat? No, because we don't have enough pig farms nearby to send it to, and our garbage has so much paper, plastic, glass and metals in it that it would injure the pigs if they ate it.

6. Could you build something to hold the garbage so the molds could eat it little by little? There is composting equipment that will do just that, and within three or four days, but we would still have all the bottles, cans and plastic, plus a large pile of compost to get rid of every day.

7. Could the wine bottles be cut in half and used for glasses? Yes, but this is usually done at home as a hobby. There are far too many bottles thrown away every day to use them all for glasses. And when the wine bottle glasses are thrown away, we still have to get rid of them.

> Very truly yours,
> Gerald J. Clarke
> Project Coordinator

Mr. Clarke has taken the questions in order, repeated them and answered them in a serious way. The children are free to ask any question at all, even if it appears to be silly.

In the following letter, Mr. Clarke expands on his earlier letter to describe the garbage situation in Westchester County. In this stage of the children's problem solving, he is giving the children information they didn't necessarily ask for. He knows they will need some background if they are to come up with real and workable solutions to the problem. The experience of learning in this way is the same as that of an adult who begins to do formal research and finds out the questions are more complicated than he originally thought.

Dear Second Graders,

This month, weather permitting, you will see an up-to-date version of the oldest form of solid waste disposal practiced by man. Do you know what that is? Throwing it away. Throwing it on the ground.

Ever since man has had something he no longer wanted, he just threw it away. Whether it was an old arrow, a pot, a broken toy, clothing or the remains of a meal, the easiest way to get rid of it was to throw it away; and he's been doing it ever since.

In the early days, the trash used to collect in the cave where he lived, and when there was no more room in the cave for him and the trash, one of them had to go. So he moved. When he began to live with others in a group, the trash was piled up outside his tent or hut, and when the garbage began to decay and smell, he covered it with dirt or dug a hole and buried it. Again, when the smell of garbage and waste got too strong the whole tribe moved. Later, when towns and cities were built and people didn't want to keep moving away from their garbage and trash, they started moving the garbage and trash away from them to the countryside where it was dumped in one big pile instead of a lot of little ones. The unpleasant look and the odor were still there, but since it was in a place where it didn't bother the people in the towns, nobody seemed to care. To this day, dumping has been the easiest and least expensive way to dispose of solid waste.

Lately, however, we've found that although it may be the easiest and the least expensive, it is definitely not the best. And possibly when we consider the long term effects of what some of these dumps are doing to our water supply, it may be the worst method of disposing of solid waste. But this is not to say that our solid waste cannot still be piled on the ground for disposal. With proper engineering and design, we can still place our solid waste in a pile and not have it pollute our streams and drinking water. This is called a sanitary landfill, and Westchester County's Croton Landfill which you will visit is one of these. We do have a problem though. We are running out of landfill space and we have no other landfill in which to put the solid waste. So we must find another method of disposal.

In seeking the answer to our problem, we must consider several very important facts.

1. There are approximately 900,000 people living in Westchester County.
2. In one year, those 900,000 people generate about 900,000 tons of solid waste, or one ton per person.
3. Each day the people throw away about 3,400 tons of solid waste. If this were piled on a football field, it would cover the entire field to a height of fourteen feet. You would only be able to see the tops of the goal posts.
4. Some of this solid waste is burned in large furnaces called incinerators in apartment houses.
5. The rest goes to the Croton Landfill along with all of the residue from the incinerators—that part of the solid waste that won't burn like cans, bottles and plastic.

So, here is our problem.

1. Every day Westchester County generates a very large amount of solid waste which must be disposed of that day.
2. When our landfill at Croton closes, the only place in Westchester County to take the solid waste will be the few incinerators which may still be operating.
3. These incinerators are polluting the air and have been ordered to close.

The county's proposed solution is to build two large new disposal plants, one at Grassland and one in Yonkers, which will take care of all the solid waste in the county. These plants will not only get rid of the solid waste each day, but will recover something as well. This could be steam for heating buildings or a fuel that could be used in place of oil or gas. In addition, we would also be able to save some of the metal cans and things so that they could be returned to the manufacturer for making new products.

It will take several years to build these plants but some communities have already started to help get rid of the solid waste by recycling paper, metal and glass. When these newspapers, cans and bottles are collected from the solid waste which is being thrown away, they can be sold and the money used to buy something for the community. Then, there is less to throw away. Every time you recycle your newspapers, cans and bottles, you are helping the community and saving money.

> Very truly yours,
> Gerald J. Clarke
> Project Coordinator

Mr. Clarke provided us with information and something even more precious—a partial solution we can sink our teeth into. He has suggested that we can do something to ease the garbage problem at least temporarily. We can recycle our papers, cans and bottles.

The children's interest in some mold on a crate of oranges has led them to make assumptions based on observing, comparing, classifying and summarizing. Their assumptions have been tested by the questioning of Mr. Clarke and by their classroom brainstorming sessions in which they reviewed the information and stated their opinions. Now, a solution has presented itself, and what does the solution lead to? Another problem. If the class wants to get involved, the children will have to state the problem—how to begin a recycling project—and go through the entire problem-solving process again.

In much the same way, we blend the skills in the curriculum into the classroom activities. Weaving in the curriculum is simply one more problem to be solved. Connecting math, reading, social studies, science and language tasks to the theme leads to the biggest continuous series of problem-solving exercises the class faces. If the children didn't practice the thinking skills from the very first day of school, they could never make the connections. They have to be told what the curriculum tasks are, of course, and it is their job to figure out how to fit them in. It is my job to make that possible, to keep the talking and thinking and brainstorming moving and to keep track of the skills to be mastered. When problems lead to newer and bigger problems, the learning never stops.

CHAPTER 6

Connecting the Curriculum

The curriculum guide, referred to in some school districts as Scope and Sequence, contains the information we say we want the children to know at particular age and grade levels. Tiny, separate skills are listed under larger categories, which in turn are listed according to subject area. The skills are disconnected from each other. Consequently, the traditional method of instruction is to maintain that separateness. Teachers move through the Scope and Sequence, teaching each skill until it is learned. They reinforce learning with examples from books or workbooks and then test for mastery. Plan books describe the way in which each skill will be taught.

Emphasis is placed on knowing, rather than thinking. The teacher knows the information before presenting it to the child. The children know the information before going to the next grade. The teacher of the next grade knows what the child has learned in the previous grade. The Scope and Sequence has dictated, through the grades, what everyone has to know.

I like to take a larger view of Scope and Sequence. I see Scope as the extent of the mind's grasp, with room or opportunity for action or thought. Sequence is the following of one thing after another; succession or continuity; a resulting event; consequence.

The Scope and Sequence then becomes a range of understandings with an implied result. Levels of understanding are built upon levels of understanding. New information is needed and sought to move to the next level. By listening and observing how much a child knows or wants to know at a given point, a teacher can supply the necessary facts and information in a variety of supportive ways. Then the child can and will take himself to new levels of understanding and expansion. Children take responsibility for their own learning and for moving themselves forward.

The theme gives me a gradually constructed hook on which to hang each individual skill. At first, we use our interests to further our understanding of the curriculum. We bind our interests together, begin projects, individually and in groups, and move toward consensus in theme identification. As we do this, we go off in many directions, some of which will be false leads, later abandoned. In the meantime, however, we are given many opportunities to integrate the curriculum.

Oct. 7, 19—

Dear Parents,

Thanks to Mrs. Parkin for participating in writing for our newsletter. I would like parents to look at how their children learn and what it would take for them to be responsible in all areas of learning.

Integrating Social Studies and Math

In preparation for Bill coming to our room, we talked about our social studies curriculum, which deals with finding your way on a map. We used a dictionary to define the vocabulary and looked at making a distinction between boundary and border.

Bill and I previously discussed the skills we wanted included in the live learning experience.

They were: making our own compass rose, working to scale, use of rulers, area and perimeter, inches, feet and yards.

When Bill came to our class on Wednesday morning, we used a variety of sizes of graph paper. We made our first rough draft, individually and in teams, using: 1 BOX = 1 FOOT. We know that means 3 BOXES = 1 YARD. We began mapping the room.

Our ultimate objective is to be accurate. Bill is returning Friday to assist us in completing our final draft. We will write the directions for a treasure hunt for the third grade to visit us next week.

Reading and Language Arts

Many exciting story ideas come directly out of our morning clearing meeting. Some children have been working on stories for an extended period of time, developing them into chapters. They include a great deal of conversation. Two groups of children have met with me to begin the editing process in order to make their stories into a book. We are using the language skills from Scope and Sequence to support this process. Children have begun by checking for punctuations and capitals. We've learned how to use conversation in a story by putting in quotation marks.

We have groups using the required reading series and added reading material that relates to their interests. Here is an interest chart that has been changed and developed over the last few weeks. We are still not sure of our theme, but we have been investigating our interests, researching and sharing with the class. Randy has suggested that maybe these interests tie together to make a theme called "roads." We are still investigating.

KITES-PAPER		MYTHOLOGY
DOLLS, PUPPETS		AIRPLANES
VIKING SHIPS	**ROADS**	CONTROL CARS, BIKES
ANIMALS		TREASURE HUNTS
WEATHER		MOTORCYCLES-REMOTE

We have read aloud *Pegasus* and *Zucchini*, two great stories related to the interests. Several children are doing research on particular animals. Some children are building models at home.

We will be giving book reports related to our interests and our emerging theme. We are listing the places we want to visit. We have thought of Mystic Seaport in Connecticut or South Street Seaport. Any suggestions?

Jenny's father, a policeman, visited our classroom and responded to questions about accidents, particularly with motorcycles, bikes and cars. The children saw the importance of wearing helmets, elbow and knee pads; we are covering the safety elements in our curriculum.

I have requested that the children ask you to read to them or listen to them read. We will be incorporating words from their independent reading into our regular second grade spelling lists.

Rachel, a SUNY-Purchase college student, finds mapping sentences fun and is planning to tell us how she does it. It is called diagramming, and she will relate that kind of mapping to our other work with maps.

Science

Part of our science curriculum deals with changes on our earth, brought about by weather or natural phenomena such as earthquakes or volcanos. We are relating these changes to our roads interest, and assuming that experts have to know about these things before they plan where to put the roads. We will look into it.

I am constantly looking at ways to blend in the skills, in a live learning experience, so the children will not only master the skills, but own them to use again in any context.

Please join us and Sara Miller at the White Plains Library Monday evening for our third parent/child/teacher partnership meeting. We will include brainstorming our interest chart to refine the theme identification, and locate the books to connect the curriculum.

Sincerely,

Elaine Young

P.S. The second partnership meeting, attended by students, parents, and teacher, was held on Sept. 21. The chairman of the math department explained that Harrison is implementing a new math curriculum. He excited parents and students when he explained his mapping experiences and suggested that mapping might be one way to include the math skills and other second grade material in a practical and fun manner.

The idea of integrating student interests with required curricula was emphasized and will continue to develop at an informal meeting at the White Plains Library next week. Several exciting threads seem to be emerging. My personal hope is that the children will see that their interests relate to "school stuff" and that the year's required studies will take on personal meaning for them.

A parent

As it turned out this year, the children could not connect all of their interests to a "road" theme. They were all pretty firmly entrenched in their dedication to their own ideas, and, while they were happy with some connections, they were dissatisfied with others. It took the broad category of "city" to make them feel as if they could participate in the central theme without letting go of their own interests. They decided to build a city in miniature form. By the time they came to that consensus, they were already in the midst of an unrelated whole-class project, the creation and presentation of a play based on *The Lemming Condition*.

Jan. 10, 19—

Dear Parents,

Happy January! We're in the midst of some exciting projects and I thought this a perfect time to show you more clearly how the skills needed by second graders are involved and how they stick because of being experienced rather than just heard and mimicked. Through planning a city, working on our book and completing the script for our play, we're covering our Scope and Sequence with a vengeance. Here's what we're covering now.

Planning a City

Math—   measurements (includes numbers 1 to 60,000,000. We measure books, pencils, scizzors, staplers, and use rulers with inches and centimeters) geometry and shapes, two and three dimensional

Social Studies—   organization of a community, reading and making maps, keys and symbols

Science—   weather, environmental factors such as pollution, liquids and solids

Reading and
Language Arts—   library books, spelling lists of "city" words

Our book

Reading and language arts—creative writing, editing, spelling, alphabetizing, knowing the parts of a book; e.g., glossary, index plus the pure fun of being published!

The Script

Reading and language arts—comprehension, story sequence, details in story, characterization, listening and speaking skills.

Science—numbers of animals (4 million lemmings, no less, and 4000 miles of ocean), animal communities.

All projects include ongoing work on word attack skills—identifying *ur, ar,* and *or* words. *Ur* words came easily when we were discussing roads; e.g. curve, turn.

This month's homework will include Shape Hunts (remember geometry?), bringing in photos and samples of two dimensional and three dimensional objects. Our spelling lists will be developed from our writing and projects, and will include a base required list plus additional words for challenge.

Happy Hunting,
Elaine Young

Whether the task is building a city, figuring out where to put the garbage or computing how many ghost trees you can put in a fantasy forest, the skills can be integrated. Learning comes as they need to understand how to do something. Each new fact presents new questions, which lead to new facts in the hierarchy of learning. It is a process of discovery.

When I ask children to tell me what they want to do, I will help them find the tools, as will their classmates who know how. There is an appropriate moment to learn everything. When learning is part of a theme development, the children see the importance of working together and sharing their skills to further the stated goals of the group—like building a city.

I confess there are times when I have to set up a situation which will lend itself to the teaching of certain skills. For example, it is a lot easier to fit a government section into a "city" theme than it is into an "insects" theme. The children might not readily see the connection in the latter case. We would want to compare (one of our thinking words again) insect communities with people communities and talk about how they both have "rules." We have already learned that things are more alike than they are different.

Planning becomes essential; even before the school year starts, I think about the curriculum. My summer phone calls to parents and students give me clues to some of the children's interests. I try to relate those interests to areas in the curriculum. "Matthew likes bikes. Perhaps we can weave in math work with miles and distance." "Stephanie's father's maps will be perfect for our mapping units."

I read and review the required curriculum guide (Scope and Sequence) for the local community. I reread the district textbooks and mark the chapters and sections which correlate to particular parts of the curriculum. I make a check list out of copies of the curriculum guide, which names each skill individually within the content areas, so there is no chance of missing anything even if topics are not covered in order. Last, I think of the curriculum as I arrange my room.

Just as the room arrangement models the thinking skills, so does it suggest the curriculum. The math corner contains the Cuisenaire rods and math games, plus any representation of the children's interests, brought in by them or me. The science table contains ordinary elements of nature—rocks, branches, dried insects and cocoons—plus items connected with predicting weather, like a barometer. Caitlin's bones would have made a perfect addition to the science table. The bulletin boards illustrate favorite stories and topics, connected with social studies, reading and language arts.

OUR CUBBY NUMBER STORIES

THE GIRLS HAVE :

12 CUBBIES AND
5 HAVE NAMES AND
7 DO NOT HAVE NAMES

THE BOYS HAVE :

12 CUBBIES AND
8 HAVE NAMES AND
4 DO NOT HAVE NAMES

THESE ARE THE RELATED NUMBER STORIES
WITHOUT WORDS .

$7 + 5 = 12$

$5 + 7 = 12$

$12 - 7 = 5$

$12 - 5 = 7$

$4 + 8 = 12$

$12 - 8 = 4$

$8 + 4 = 12$

$12 - 4 = 8$

WHAT NUMBER IS MISSING IN EACH STORY ?

[12 , 5 , 7]

$7 + \square = 12$

$5 + \square = 12$

$\square - 7 = 5$

$\square - 5 = 7$

(12 , 4 , 8]

$\square + 8 = 12$

$12 - 8 = \square$

$\square + 4 = 12$

$12 - 4 = \square$

RETELL THE NUMBER STORIES
USING WORDS .

CLASS 2Y

As the year begins, the children will walk into a room filled with their interests, arranged to reinforce both the curriculum and the thinking skills. As they enter, I invite them to look around the room. Some of them were present to help me set up the room in the summer. Others are seeing it for the first time. I ask them to identify the things in the room which they brought in or which relate to their interests. We then have our first clearing meeting.

The clearing meeting begins each day. It is a time for building trust and problem solving, a time for sharing and brainstorming about connections—between individuals and groups in the classroom, between interests and projects, between thinking skills and curriculum. On the first day of school, as we talk about what we will accomplish that day, problems arise concerning seating arrangements and distribution of cubbies. At the same time as I begin the thinking and problem-solving process, I also turn our cubby dilemma into a math exercise.

I try to include at least one textbook or workbook exercise on the first day of school, so that the children can work in a way that is familiar to them. When they do their paper and pencil work, I let them do it the way they are used to, so that their own questions arise, such as, "Did I do this right?" or "Should I print or write?" I also try to stick to the order agreed upon at the clearing meeting. From time to time during the year, we will become engrossed in a particular project and will want to change from the order agreed upon in the morning clearing meeting; but at least the first day of school, it is important for the children to have the security of knowing what will happen.

During that first clearing meeting, I distribute a brand new notebook to each child. More than a diary or journal, the record book provides an opportunity to jot down individual thoughts, drawings, scribbles, plans, anything that doesn't fit into the rest of the day. I make it clear that the record is each child's personal property, and he or she may share it or keep it private.

In those first few days, we develop our first interest chart and try to make connections between our interests. We also connect each interest to the major curriculum areas. This year, roads were identified early as a major interest.

MATHEMATICS	SCIENCE
measuring, geometry	effects of weather
building materials	

ROADS

SOCIAL STUDIES	READING and LANGUAGE ARTS
other cultures	poetry and stories about traveling
	writing about where roads can
	take us

We learn that just as the clearing meeting gives us a good feeling about our direction for the day, so does our recap of the day at the end. Each day, I distribute a simple time management chart to each child. Under "What I accomplished today," I ask the students to list the activities they worked on, in just a word or two. Under "What I learned today," they mention the skill they mastered. Under "What I'm still working on," they mention work in progress. Since completing these charts can be a difficult and time consuming task for beginning second graders, I don't ask for meticulous work. The charts are to refresh our memories, so we can share out loud what we have accomplished.

During that first week, I also write down at least a few descriptive words about how each child learns and what his or her interests appear to be. I pay particular attention to what seems to attract the children and what their learning style might be. How do they work—alone, in a group, silently, verbally, visually, numerically? By the end of the week, when it is time for me to plan for the next week, I have a tentative direction for each child, and I have established some possibilities for reading groups.

> Caitlin and Karie—don't want to read aloud—like to move ahead in their reading by themselves.
> Karie—cried when she made a mistake—work on risk-taking as act of growth.
> Barry—knows all the major dinosaurs—have him do bulletin board on prehistoric animals.
> Natalie and Randy—like poetry—way to help Natalie with her reading.

Esther—will bring in pictures of her life in Israel—feels comfortable with Bible stories as reading.

Matthew—brought in a shoe box—have him develop project for next week—share it at clearing meeting. (Watch—may have reading problems.)

Fred—do something with his monster pictures. What?—quick at understanding numbers—class banker?

Jay—said, "Last night I had a dream and I thought everybody hated my story"—work on this.

Corey—hasn't talked—writes sensitively—acknowledge writing—call Mom.

Ryan, Jeremy, Stephanie—will work on projects independently and at length—call Stephanie's father about visiting this Wednesday.

Janine—"I read when I get up in the middle of the night, a lot of times"—ask others how reading fits into their lives.

Tentative reading groups:
> Karie and Caitlin
> Ryan, Jay, Corey and Jeremy
> Randy, Fred, Barry, Janine and Stephanie
> Matthew and Natalie
> individual—Esther

Every weekend, I begin my planning by making these brief notes about the children, documenting their learning in the previous week. When I do this, I am helped by their simple time management plans and their own reactions to the class as we close each day. I then develop an overall plan of action for the following week. Again, I keep my work sketchy. It is important that most of my energy goes to working with the children and being with them in a way that will cause them to grow.

Plan of action—week of Sept. 10 to 14

Begin to identify outside resources that will help us learn more about our interests. Start with Stephanie's father and the Hutchinson River Parkway maps. That will further the road interest and connect it to the mapping part of the curriculum. He has agreed to come in on Wednesday. Plan with the children to prepare for the visitor. Practice assuming and developing questions. Identify academic areas related to mapping. Look for related newspaper articles and bring them in. Develop words connected with roads.

Record books

Observe which children persist in writing. Ask Randy and Natalie to share their enthusiasm for poetry during clearing meeting. Get it to spread. Read a poem during morning discussion. For children who are mainly drawing in their record books, ask them to illustrate each drawing with at least three words.

Publish our first newsletter. Involve Corey.

Don't push too hard with the road interest. The first interest chart indicated other interests, too. Do some skills with bike words. Think about the dolls and puppets mentioned by Karie. Call puppet and doll maker in New York. Invite him in to speak.

Begin planning for first publication—record book excerpts for parents. Work to make the piece "look good." Observe which children are willing to redo their work—Ryan, Jeremy, Stephen—and ask them to begin.

After I have completed my notes about what I would like to accomplish in general, I finish my plan book, working from the curriculum areas. Sometimes, I break the week down into days, for projects and assignments that are clearly defined and of short duration. Other times, I work in two or three day or even week-long segments.

Week of Sept. 10-14

Mathematics

Monday—Take off on cubby worksheets to continue concept of sets. Odds and evens. Use dittos. Review addition and subtraction, predicting odd and even numbers. Count by twos. Hand out red math books to children who seem to work creatively with numbers. Have Fred work with others. Janine needs help.

Tuesday—Teach concept of measurement, inches, feet and yards, in preparation for visit by Stephanie's father. See if we can make a yard with finger and string.

Wednesday—Prepare questions about measuring and mapping for Stephanie's father.

Thursday and Friday—Set up math lab materials with teacher's guide for open house. As a follow up to Stephanie's father's visit, begin mapping skills. Measure carpet in library. Use graph paper, 1 FOOT = 1 SQUARE, to begin relief maps.

Social Studies

Monday—Have Esther show pictures of Israel. Notice similarities and differences in our countries. Look at maps of both countries. Discuss how terrain can influence culture. Relate to Stephanie's father coming on Wednesday. Ask Barry if he will tell the class about Iran. Involve Karie and Caitlin—dolls from other countries.

Tuesday—Think of all the things we can map. The classroom, our yards, cities. Compare different kinds of maps and make assumptions about the people who make them. Share *New York Times* article, "Map to Ship's Treasure." Ryan is interested because his neighbor was on the *Andrea Doria*. Make treasure maps.

Wednesday—Stephanie's father visits. Develop questions about the people who are the bosses of making roads—state government.

Thursday and Friday—Discuss Stephanie's father's visit. Who is the big boss of state roads? Why did our roads get taken over by the state instead of the county? Develop questions for Governor Cuomo about the Hutchinson River Parkway problem. Write to him.

Science

Monday and Tuesday—Discuss dinosaurs, large prehistoric animals. Read aloud "Patrick's Dinosaurs." Use Barry as a resource. Begin bulletin board in hall. Jay has suggested large dinosaur eating children's school work as a theme. That way we can display everyone's work.

Wednesday—Develop science questions for Stephanie's father. Ask about safety with bikes and motorcycles on the roads.

Thursday and Friday—Examine rock core samples brought in by Stephanie's father. Make assumptions about how the cracks and holes get in the roads. Relate to the effects of weather on man-made materials. Houses? Schools?

Reading
To be covered during the week

Karie and Caitlin—Complete "Dragon in the Clock Boy" and related workbook pages. Encourage them to read aloud to each other, for purposes of improving expression. They would rather read ahead to themselves.

Ryan, Jay, Corey and Jeremy—Complete "The Giant" and related workbook pages. They like to complete their workbooks right away. Encourage them to read other materials related to their interests.

Randy, Fred, Barry, Janine and Stephanie—Complete "The Giant" carefully. Have children repeat in their own words the workbook directions. Limit assignments and check.

Matthew and Natalie—Like to read aloud with me. Read along in *Being Me*. Cannot hear *nt* and *nd* endings of words. Refer Matthew to L.D. teacher for testing.

Read aloud to the children *The Lemming Condition*. Listen for the possibility of turning it into a play.

Have discussion about how the children feel about reading—out loud, to themselves, on their own, at home.

Language Arts
Monday—Identify clues on maps that show how to read them. Introduce North, South, East, West as concepts. Look for related newspaper articles. Make signs needed for relief maps.

Tuesday—Have children begin to select work from their record books that they wish to have in their first publication. Plan format with children. Assist in reworking poems for visual effect. Do something with Fred's monster pictures—maybe write stories for him as he dictates them. Learn about editing and making things better. Look for typist to type up children's stories.

Wednesday—Ask questions about words we don't understand from Stephanie's father's talk.

Thursday and Friday—Write thank you letters to Stephanie's father. Make stories about what we learned about the Hutchinson River Parkway. Begin letters to Governor Cuomo. Have those children who are interested in dolls and puppets begin working on a puppet show.

Spelling
During the week

Alphabetize road words, using first, second, third and sometimes fourth letter. Identify consonant blends at beginning, middle and end of words.

I continually monitor myself to see whether we, as a class, have mastered the skills to be learned, and I remind myself of the skills yet to be covered. I do not become distressed if what is planned for a given day does not occur, but in a given week I know what I intend to accomplish with the class. The details depend on the applicability to our interests and our theme.

I have to make absolutely certain that all of the skills in the curriculum are covered, so I keep a check list, on which I note the introduction of and reinforcement of each item. This is an easier task than it might seem. I simply photocopy the pages in the curriculum guide, several times if necessary. Each time we work on a project which touches on a given skill, I simply jot down the date next to the skill, so that I can refer back to my plan book if I want to know what I did. Of course, the children have contact with each skill numerous times throughout the year, until it is really theirs.

In order to illustrate how the skills are taught through attentiveness to interests, development of projects and connection to the theme, I have extracted excerpts from my plan book, and correlated them with skills in the Scope and Sequence. Notice how each activity relates to more than one curriculum area.

Scope and Sequence

Plan Book Excerpts

Reading and Language Arts
Determine number of syllables
in one, two and three syllable
words. Listen for specific
information. Understand the
importance of listening.
Participate in class discussion.

Barry's father sent in a map of Iran.
Compare it to Esther's map of
Israel. Look for identifying marks.
Compare the two countries, geo-
graphically and politically. Invite
Barry's father and Esther's mother in
to talk with us.

Social Studies
Identify the concept of a community.
Compare and contrast various
kinds of communities. Classify
differences and similarities among
communities. Analyze character of
communities. Identify key to a map.
Identify directions. Differentiate
longitude/latitude.

Science
Understand factors related to
weather changes and how these
can be determined. List at least
three factors that help to make up
the weather.

Social Studies
Compare and contrast various
kinds of communities, including
farms, cities, towns. Locate their
community on a map. Identify
directions, N.S.E.W.

continued on next page

Scope and Sequence

Plan Book Excerpts

Reading and Language Arts
Find main idea. Draw conclusions. Predict outcomes. Determine cause and effect. Listen for specific information. Participate in class discussions. Write an asking sentence, using a capital letter at the beginning and a question mark at the end. Write a note and identify its parts: greeting, body, closing, signature.

Invite Stephanie's father to show maps of Hutchinson River Parkway. He will review three maps: the land before the Parkway was built, the land as it is now and the way it will look after the proposed construction.
Prepare questions, and write thank you notes following his visit.

Mathematics
Recite amount in inches, feet, centimeters, meters. Measure length to nearest 1/2 inch or centimeter. Distinguish between open and closed figures. Locate and name positions on grid.

Social Studies
Compare communities in different times and places. Classify differences in provision of food, clothing and shelter.

continued on next page

Scope and Sequence

Science

Collect and/or draw at least three pictures of animals that eat plants. Understand the similarities and differences between natural communities. List at least three conditions that characterize a specific community. When given an example of over-population, predict at least two possible effects on plants and animals.

Reading and Language Arts

Find main idea. Develop story sequence. Identify details in story. Distinguish between fact and fiction. Draw conclusions. Recognize fables and folktales. Read stories for enjoyment. Understand the importance of listening. Follow oral and written directions. Read and enjoy good literature. Write correctly book titles and story titles, using capital letters where needed.

Mathematics

Identify a set as a group of numbers. Write numbers in order from 0-999. Differentiate between even and odd sets. Identify sum as the addition of two numbers. Use addition to solve word problems.

Plan Book Excerpts

Tie in our reading of *The Lemming Condition* with other kinds of mapping. Developing character and plot are kinds of mapping. Connect with the ways we report about roads, countries, animals, bones. Use bones Dr. Purdey brings in to chart things that are alive and not alive. Classify bones by size, hardness, use. Find ways to map out findings.

As I plan for each child in connection with his or her interests, or in relation to the theme, I create assignments from texts, workbooks and independent research that will address the skill to be mastered. Sometimes assignments are given to the whole class, sometimes to a group working on a particular project and sometimes to an individual.

I insist that the children are able to identify the skill they are working on: that they are able to speak the term, describe it, and use it in connection with their interests. I ask that those children who have mastered the skill serve as resources for others. When an individual or group has learned a new skill, I call the class together in a discussion group with a blackboard handy and have the experts share what they learned. It is not always the same children who are the teachers/coaches. Everyone can feel proud of success in some area. Information and skills become knowledge learned, relearned and then taught to someone else.

Our guest speakers fill in the gaps. I may use a visitor/expert to get us started on a topic, or I may invite a guest to make a connection for us—between our interest and part of the curriculum. I tell the visitor what the students need to master, as well as what interests them.

I ask the students to keep track of their own learning through their time management plans. Instead of looking at progress by test scores, we can see how, when and where the children are able to move to the new levels of understanding.

We do have to test, of course, because accountability is important; but wherever possible, we test at our convenience. When it seems like a particular skill has been mastered, I test judiciously, in small or whole group situations. I try to use the results positively, to identify areas to work on. Consequently, when standardized tests have to be administered in unison with the rest of the school, the children have developed the self-confidence to handle the tests with minimal anxiety, and they usually do quite well.

As the year ends, we review by brainstorming what we have learned, what we are good at and how we have grown. We tie up any loose ends in the curriculum and talk about the years ahead. We make assumptions about what school will be like next year and list ways in which we can use what we have learned in a different situation, with a different teacher, different classmates and different subject matter. The children know that they have grown in knowledge and understanding. They can remember and store facts to be used again when the connections and necessity present themselves. More importantly, they know that whatever they don't know, they can find out. They can organize information, ask questions, make assumptions and draw their own conclusions. They have become lifetime learners.

CHAPTER 7

Unfolding

When you combine classroom preparation, listening to the children, building trust and sharing feelings, you have opened the door to lifetime learning. Focusing on individual interests, consolidating those interests into a theme and weaving in the thinking skills and curriculum all make that learning solid.

I call my work a curriculum for self-esteem. It is a genuine curriculum in that the process is planned and deliberate and can be described; yet, it promotes self-esteem because it is not the same for everyone. It takes into account individual strengths and interests. It allows the children to choose.

As children experience choice, they begin to see the benefits and burdens associated with their decisions.

The paths they travel will be ones of not knowing, but discovering. As they change with their choices, the energy flows within them, and they unfold. They are renewed to continue learning, perhaps in a different way. They never go back to the beginning. They start from where they are. The unfolding goes on and on, taking its energy from within and without, in self-trust and sharing with others.

My friend Misao and I took a walk to look at all of the unfolding in life. I thought about how I have unfolded in writing this book. I thought about how families and students unfold. I passed a fence with roses climbing on it. Most of the roses were dead or nearly dead. At the bottom of the fence, though, all alone by itself, was one rose: bright, alive, attached to the stalk, with a crack in one leaf. I wondered—how did it survive when all of the others had died? Where did it get its strength? Why didn't the other roses have the strength to blossom like that? Did they all get the same nourishment? What made this one rose unfold and stay open in all of its strength? What would it be like if all of the roses had that same strength of endurance?

Then I noticed along a second fence were several clusters of shoots that had beautiful roses unfolded all together, each on a small strong stem. I thought I knew why that particular plant had produced so many lovely clusters, and the other plant had only a single rose: care, nourishment and the chance to be the best it could be.

Misao described unfolding as breathing and sharing life. The trees need to breathe the carbon dioxide we exhale. In turn, they give us the oxygen that we need to breathe. She said that is why the early morning air is so full of oxygen for us to take in. She described the cut flowers she arranges as being alive, as needing water to keep living. She even believes the plants need us to talk to them. We need each other, plants and humans, to live. Living things, when they give to each other, nourish themselves and cause their own unfolding.

The images people have in their minds to describe the unfolding are as different as people are unique. I see unfolding in terms of gentle roses. Misao thinks of plants and animals as unfolding when they exchange oxygen and carbon dioxide.

One parent described the process in more explosive terms. She said it seemed as if we (the class) had blasted a hole in a mountain, to make the mountain receptive to learning. Now we would need to support the opening with two-by-fours.

To continue her analogy, children who have awakened to a feeling of self-worth are exposed to learning as the open mountain is exposed to the environment. The continued opportunities for sharing are the two-by-fours that keep the opening intact. The elements will encroach upon the opening, covering it from time to time. But the earth is soft and ready. The opening of self-esteem can be made wider again by new experiences of enrichment.

Whether likened to roses, or air or holes in a mountain, the feeling of acquiring self-esteem is both unique to each individual and the same.

I designed the following questionnaire so I could discover the ways my students and their parents described that feeling. This is not a scientific survey, but rather a collection of reactions to a single classroom experience. I invited 130 families to respond to my questions and received 30 returns. Needless to say, some of my students were more enchanted with their second grade experience than others. Reading and responding to their reaction, and the reactions of their parents, proved to be a valuable lesson for me—another adventure in my own quest for lifetime learning.

THE QUESTIONNAIRE

1. When your child, _____, returned home from school during the 19__ to __ school year, how would you generally describe his/her state of mind, his/her attitude toward the day's activities?

2. Did your child discuss with you the activities in which he/she participated while in Mrs. Young's class? How would you characterize these discussions?

3. How would you describe your child's growth intellectually in Mrs. Young's class? Socially? Emotionally?

4. Was your child prepared to enter the next grade after a year in Mrs. Young's class? If not, what shortcomings did your child experience?

5. When your child was preparing to go to school in the morning, how would you generally characterize his/her attitude or state of mind?

6. If there was one thing you wish Mrs. Young had done differently, what would that be?

7. Was there a particular class event or activity (or series of events or activities) which you felt was or were outstanding with respect to positive effects on your child?

8. Have you ever recommended or not recommended to another parent Mrs. Young as a teacher for your child? Why or why not?

9. If your child would like to say something about his/her experiences in Mrs. Young's class, would you please allow him or her to do so at this point?

Since, as I mentioned, this is not a scientific survey, I have organized the responses into the categories of self-esteem, sharing feelings, interests, activities and projects, teacher attitude and academic expectations. In that way, we are better able to detect themes and patterns in the reactions of those who answered the questionnaire. The responses of both parents and children are included in each category.

SELF-ESTEEM

"Elaine Young has an uncanny knack for making her students feel that they are the brightest, most talented children she has ever known. My son was still busy talking and interrupting the class whenever he had something to say and instead of scolding him, she would let him know that what he was saying was making an important contribution to the class; however, he should raise his hand and not interrupt whoever was speaking because they too had something important to contribute. As he came to trust Elaine more and more, he knew that anything he had to contribute would be well received by both her and his classmates because, unknown to the children, she had been building up all of their self-confidence and their trust of each other. This spilled over to their academics as well because my son was no longer afraid of failure because in Elaine's class there is no such word."

"Prior to Mrs. Young's class, he hated school."

"Still in all, the reason I love and respect Elaine Young most is that she gave my son a tremendous sense of self-esteem and importance that I don't think will ever be equalled again."

"Self-esteem was high—sometimes too high!"

"This year encouraged his self-esteem and made participating with other children very easy."

"It was a year that Johnny made an amazing growth in his self-esteem."

"In Mrs. Young's class, he developed a positive self-image and became a lot more confident in himself."

"A sense of accomplishment and achievement. Also showed in his desire to share new ideas. Confident."

"She shared experiences with classmates and Mrs. Young, and therefore grew confident in herself, socially and emotionally."

"He felt very good about himself."

"Both of my children who attended Elaine's class seemed content, happy and pleased with themselves."

"When I think of my son's second grade experience, the words 'feel good' come to mind, both for him and for myself."

SHARING FEELINGS

"She (Elaine) taught them the difference from right and wrong. How to care for others but to be firm in their convictions without feeling guilty about their decision. She taught creativity, how to explore from within, not to harbor their feelings but how to share them."

"The discussion on divorce comes to my mind, any children with thoughts on or experience with divorce shared their experiences. My son was affected by these discussions. At times, he was upset, but I think that exposure to the thoughts and emotions of these children helped him to deal with them. I also think it will help him deal with difficult issues in his everyday life."

"It was a good year of growth—feelings became important."

"Dawn learned to care about and get involved with other people. By sharing with others, she went through a lot of different emotions during the year. It was positive."

"The children are encouraged to see the whole world about them and express in their own way feelings that they feel about people, things and experiences."

"The activity and perhaps the single most important was one sharing time which taught children that other feelings were important, relevant and interesting. Edgar learned to communicate."

and—one student's reaction

"She was very much into humanitarianism. When Mrs. H. died, we all learned a lot about death from her. She was a very good teacher."

INTERESTS

"He overcame a tremendous obstacle with your encouragement, and you sparked an interest in cartooning."

"I think the whole basis of teaching around a common interest theme made the year one which truly turned Johnny onto learning facts and in turn sharing them in the form of trivia games at home. His growth was truly astounding."

"Don did feel important that he had information on Indians, from his grandma, that helped the class."

"Daniel was involved with experimenting with fruit flies, nature, Hook Mountain, garbage dumps. He discussed it all with enthusiasm."

"I could see how focused her lessons were and marvelled in the delightful way she has of leading the class to the focal point from so many different angles, which, in my opinion, taught them so much more and so interestingly. To me, that's what teaching is all about. Who can really learn if they aren't interested?"

"Mrs. Young's ability to draw her students out and make them interested in everything going on around them."

ACTIVITIES AND PROJECTS

"The *Zucchini* play was an outstanding experience for my son. He had three different parts to learn for the play. One of the parts he requested; the other two, he acquired. He was a little nervous about handling the lines for all the parts. He told me he wasn't sure he could do it, so I told him to talk to Mrs. Young. She was convinced that he could 'do it all' and he sensed that by her enthusiasm. He did perform all three parts, and his self-confidence skyrocketed. She believed in him, so he believed in himself."

"Writing a play and then producing it—an invaluable process."

"The children put on a play, on a book they read. Dawn was very excited and involved. I don't think she will ever forget it."

"The writing done in this class was a vehicle through which Erma blossomed. She learned to read through it, she was motivated to stretch and learn. The play was also a very positive experience with a slight flaw—she seemed to have a gigantic 'I'm the best ever' attitude."

"A frequent invitation of outside experts to talk to in class played a very positive role. This was unique. My child talked for weeks about these experiences."

"Each child kept a notebook and wrote in it daily—stories, poems, thoughts, pictures—positively the child's own creation. This taught confidence in expressing oneself on an emotional and intellectual (second grade) level. Freedom of creativity was greatly encouraged. She is graduating high school this June and writes beautifully today."

"Poetry reading and creative working—these were Edgar's favorite activities and he delighted in giving me daily progress reports."

"I think the school play was a wonderful experience for my child last year."

"He discussed the class activities in detail (the radio show and the class play) and with great animation."

"Yes, he often talked about some of the activities that went on. I would say these discussions were always very enthusiastic."

"You helped him so much by encouraging participation and cultivating the children's ideas, that he did exchange ideas and develop friendships early on in the year."

"My child was usually happy and excited about whatever project or activity took place."

and—from the children's perspective—

"Science project evolving around electricity in which there developed a lot of poetry and essays."

"When two princesses were allowed to perform the school play—also, the acting out of books and characters."

"Building castles in the block corner."

"The school play had a very positive effect on me. It helped in giving confidence."

"I enjoyed Mrs. Young's class. I liked the castle projects and working at a parent's shop. I liked reading poems and stories aloud. I liked the play, *Zucchini*. I liked doing the book-making. Everything was fun about Mrs. Young's class."

"I really enjoyed being in Mrs. Young's class, especially since there was always some special project or happening during the course."

"I loved everything we did in Mrs. Young's. I liked writing the best of all. I'm writing a story that I'm hoping can be published. I've written about a flying land. I learned how to write good stories and now I'm better at writing. I liked the trips we went on too, even though I got burrs in my hair on the trip to Manhattanville College."

"There were many school plays, discussion groups, etc. Tom Edison play comes to mind."

"The play, *The Lion, the Witch, and the Wardrobe*, and the class trips which we took."

"The best part of Mrs. Young's was story time."

"The class play, the radio program, building the kibbutz, bringing in books on subjects of interest; warm class atmosphere."

Children's Attitudes

"Edgar thought school was fun and genuinely enjoyed class activities. He always had a very positive feeling, quite unlike his feelings from the year before. Prior to Mrs. Young's class, he hated school."

"My child always came home in a relaxed mood and proud of the day's accomplishments."

"My child always looked forward to going to school."

"He always looked forward to going to school and was very happy there."

"She always told us it was a very easy class, but she learned to love reading, and she still does today."

"She often shared her writing and information about the *Zucchini* play. She was pleased and proud of what she did."

"Looked forward to going. Things to do and people to be with."

"Sometimes eager, sometimes unhappy. She did not like the fact that there were not assigned desks. Also, if the special subject area being stressed was not to her liking, she was inclined to complain."

"She was very enthusiastic about the activities."

"She would discuss the day with enthusiasm."

"My child was eager to share what went on in class."

"Looked forward to the next day."

"A very healthy outlook. Relaxed, pleased and very comfortable."

"Yes, he was excited. Alan loved his day's activities."

"Felt concern over the fact that she was able to work by herself—she wanted to work as a whole class—and missed this."

"The independence of a classroom such as Mrs. Young's allows a child to develop responsibility well before his time."

and—from the children—

"I had a lot of fun in Mrs. Young's class."

"I was very happy in your class. Although it didn't seem like I learned a lot. Maybe I did. Anyway, I had fun. I wish you were my teacher again."

"I remember the class as being fun and well behaved in which I learned a great deal, which helped me in my later years at Purchase School."

"It was FUN!"

TEACHER ATTITUDE

"As my daughter said, 'she's the only teacher who learns along with you.'"

"Because I feel that Mrs. Young concerned herself more than most with developing the undisciplined child's wish to learn and grow and become. My daughter did not improve Mrs. Young's way—Mrs. Young worked my daughter's way. It might not work for everyone."

"An atmosphere of support, love, safety and whatever else her magic is."

"Her human touch. Her personal attention and care. Her concern for others."

"She was nice. She aroused sufficient curiosity in her students. She was considerate and she took good care of every individual in the class. She was compassionate."

"I have great faith in the way Mrs. Young took care of her class. Once when I was in her class, I found how students were encouraged to ask questions. They were open and very receptive to ideas. They were very original."

"I remember Mrs. Young's class most for her ability to know each child and reach them in a very special, caring way. She never took the easy way out. She is a working teacher."

"She (my daughter) was given special consideration and was treated fairly."

"I appreciated the nurturing and self-confidence that was given to the boys. She has the ability to listen to the child, which is very important. She teaches in a way which the child learns without realizing he is learning."

"She knows just how to make them feel proud of themselves."

"It is most gratifying as parents to see the devotion of Mrs. Young to her students and especially our son, recognizing his individual needs."

"The newsletters she sends home, the books of poetry and stories her pupils write. These are all indications of a skilled, warm, interested and devoted educator whom I respect and admire."

"The children themselves have a deep affection for her. It is obvious without a doubt that she genuinely likes children and loves teaching. She is an extremely dedicated teacher—always searching for new ways to utilize ideas and activities. She understands children beautifully. Her ability to listen to children and pick up from them their desires, ideas, feelings, etc. is incredible. She goes beyond the scope of 'school teacher' in that she accomplishes with her class the development of many of the human characteristics and qualities we believe should emanate from the home. That is, these children are not just students; they are people. And, people—whether small or large—have feelings and ideas which should and must be heard and dealt with. Elaine Young is quality. We want quality education for our children. My son got it in spades this year and we are ecstatic."

ACADEMIC EXPECTATIONS

"I would say his growth intellectually was very rapid."

"I would much rather have had Mrs. Young's teaching method continue, but the growth he made helped him to make the transition."

"Wouldn't change a thing."

"Mrs. Young instilled a desire, purpose and most of all an internal excitement. Learning became fun and my son developed a sense of autonomy. He learned from within. There were no artificial, extrinsic rewards, there was only the sense of self desire. What a powerful source—the desire to learn from within. He was given that special gift."

"I would have liked her to spend more time on the basics. I also would have liked her to be more realistic about his attributes. Vance was very happy and had positive feelings about himself."

"My daughter, because of emotional problems connected with learning disabilities, had a hard time learning—even with the special efforts of Mrs. Young."

"I would have liked a better balance between the 3 R's and all the creative areas she concentrated on."

"Devin had problems because of a lack of structure in second grade. He needed to be pushed more. If allowed to play, that was all he would do. He did have confidence, and he seemed to catch on easily once in third grade."

"Elaine stimulated Edgar in ways he had never been stimulated before. He was encouraged to use his imagination, dare to be different and work independently at his own pace. He 'grew up' in second grade."

"Always returned home happy, but not always satisfied with the work she had done during the day."

"If a child needs structure and drill to learn the basic concepts, then I would not recommend Mrs. Young. If the child is academically sound and enjoys other subject areas to study in detail, then I would recommend her."

"I felt that all work was praised, and that it may be better to praise effort rather than the work."

"A little more emphasis on the basics—more grammar and spelling."

"Much more than the simple acquisition of skills, the child's own process of inquiry and discovery has been tapped."

"As a bright youngster, Mrs. Young encouraged his natural curiosities and introduced him to many avenues of reading. I am sure he would not have come to this for several years on his own. She was aware of his ability and I believe this was most encouraging and helpful."

"Her insight into my son's academic growth was most helpful to us as parents."

"I found her class was run with excitement and the children were always made to feel enthusiasm about whatever they were learning."

"He was encouraged to make decisions and develop opinions which he did in a very logical way."

"I believe Mrs. Young's style of classroom has done much to open the minds of her pupils. Besides achieving all skills expected of her grade, my daughter has gained a fair amount of self-confidence."

"Education, according to Webster's dictionary, is defined as 'the process of training and developing the knowledge, skills, mind, character, etc.' It is a total program, enveloping many areas. And, that is precisely the emphasis exhibited in Mrs. Young's classroom. Exploration is, or ought to be, a mandatory ingredient of quality education. The opening up of new horizons in the cultural and creative arenas; being exposed to differing and changing worlds; probing and discovering the area of self-awareness; stressing the importance of expression and sharing independent thoughts and ideas. All these things, and a great many more, Elaine Young did and did in a unique and outstanding way."

and—some reactions from the students—

"She has got to be the reason for which science is my favorite subject. Every day we did something or other in this field. My favorite part of the day was when she took time to read to us."

"I feel that I basically learned about things that I did not need for third grade."

"The activated student finds learning enjoyable under such conditions. This in turn propagates a drive and desire to continue learning. I found my classroom experience in second grade to be one of immense enjoyment. A child of age seven usually does not have a recall of his classroom experience by the time he reaches college. However, I must say I recall my experiences with Mrs. Young to be quite memorable. This is a credit to Mrs. Young and her unique teaching abilities."

As you can see, many of my students and parents came to value the investigative style of learning they became acquainted with in second grade; a few have expressed reservations about what they perceive as a lack of emphasis on the "basics." It may be true that the classroom experience my students encounter is not for everyone. I like to believe, however, that all students are changed in some small way by the chance to be loved and appreciated exactly as they are.

The self-esteem that is generated may not always seem valuable at the time it is being acquired. Children may be seen as having a good time but not learning much. But when they need to learn in other contexts, they can. They have the tools of confidence and sound technique. They know where to go to get what they need. If what they need is more structure, more routine, then that knowledge is what they take with them. They know they are free to enhance a learning style all their own.

Extracted from the responses to the questionnaire, the following are words that best describe a lifetime learner.

accomplishment	interesting
achievement	introduce
affection	involved
best	listen
blossomed	little distress
caring	logical
challenged	looking forward
comfortable	mandatory
communicate	no hesitations
compassionate	no tears
confident	opening
considerate	original
content	overcome
cooperative	participation
creates	pleased
cultivating	positive
curiosity	powerful
dedicated	probing
delighted	proud
desire	quality
discovery	receptive
eager	relaxed
encouraged	relevant
enjoyable	responsibility
excited	satisfied
fun	searching
happening	skilled
happy	source
helped	special
human	stimulated

humanitarianism	supportive
imagination	terrific
important	thrive
independent	understand
inquiring	unique
insight	utilize
	warm
	willing
	wonderful

I invite teachers and friends to be lifetime learners, and to do what I ask the children to do. Apply these invigorating adjectives to yourselves. Put yourself in an environment where you can flourish. Identify your personal interests. Develop a project. Ask for support. Collaborate with others. Set a deadline for accomplishment. Let your project unfold as you unfold with it. Stay aware of new ideas that develop as a result of your involvement. Be willing to risk getting stuck. If you meet an obstacle, find the detour. Alter the plan.

If you become a lifetime learner along with your students, if you join with them in not knowing, not being sure, the excitement of unfolding is yours as well as theirs. Unfolding children can be the teachers for unfolding parents and educators. Lifetime learning is like lifetime living. It begins with an inner energy source and grows richer in our listening and speaking.

FOR SHARON

What is a Prayer?
A rabbi said
If you haven't heard music,
How can I tell you?

What is music?
A friend said,
Music is Love.
If you haven't heard love,
How can I tell you?

What is a child?
I say
A child is a vessel
To give and receive unconditional love.
If you haven't heard a child,
How can I tell you?

Elaine Young

A Formula for the Development of Self-Esteem

We are all committed to having each and every child in our care recognize his/her own special magnificence. We are teachers or parents because we wish to encourage children to be joyous, responsible, contributing and self-confident human beings, able to affect their world. Children must have self-esteem to dare to live as fully as that. The book you have just read describes one way to help children obtain and keep self-esteem by maintaining an atmosphere where living and learning constitute a single act of growth.

In this process, there is no separation between life in and out of school, or between personal and intellectual development. There is no separation between teacher and students, except for the obvious ones related to age and experience. In the end, students become teachers and coaches; teachers become learners.

The book describes more than a method. It is an idea, carried forward by a way of being as much as doing. The focus is in the acts of listening to and questioning—the children, yourself, others—without fear, in an open manner, ever-willing to change as the moment unfolds. This kind of active listening means that something happens every time a new thought is introduced. That thought is considered in relation to those that have gone before; new action can be taken, new inquiries can be made, new research can be conducted, new conclusions can be drawn. The children know there are no limits or restrictions placed on learning or on them. They can do and think anything.

The following, therefore, is an effort to summarize and make concrete a process which is not easily reduced to a recipe. Even though this process is deliberate and contrived, it is not readily outlined in steps. In fact, the same skills of listening, questioning, brainstorming and building on interests are used over and over during the year, in ever more intricate and sophisticated fashion.

Thus, this yearly guide is simply a reference tool. At any time, the order can reverse itself, the direction can change and the plan can be abandoned or altered to allow for individual differences and to take advantage of a teachable moment.

I. DURING THE SUMMER

A. MAKE PHONE CALLS TO PARENTS

The phone calls begin the partnership of trust among parents, students and teacher.

1. Compile a list of names of children and parents, and parents' occupations.
2. Greet the person you are talking to and introduce yourself. You might begin, "Hello, I am Elaine Young, Joey's teacher this year. I am calling to say hello and get acquainted. Do you have a few minutes? Would you tell me about Joey?"
3. Be sure to ask if this is a good time. If not, schedule a time when you can call again. Extend an invitation to have the child present also, or give your number so the child can call you back.
4. Listen in a way that accepts and does not interfere with what the parents are saying.
5. Have the parents speak first. Invite them to talk about their child.
6. Encourage them to continue with leading responses.
7. Take notes about children's likes, dislikes, interests and parents' hopes for their children.
8. Invite parents to talk about their own careers and interests, and ask them how they might wish to share these interests.
9. Acknowledge the parents' sharing.
10. Let the parents know that this is the beginning of a continuing dialogue for partnership.
11. Invite them to a first parent/child/teacher partnership meeting. Give the time, place, date. Be specific.
12. End the phone call by sharing yourself. Speak about your commitment to children and what you hope to accomplish as a team.
13. Ask again about their project in education for their child, and discuss your project in education.

B. REVIEW THE CURRICULUM

The method of teaching curriculum skills at the moment when the skills match the children's interests requires meticulous record keeping, so that certain skills are not overlooked.

1. Read and review the required curriculum guide for the state and the local community.
2. Review the district textbooks.
3. Correlate the chapters in the texts to the state and local curriculum guide.
4. List the materials in your classroom that reinforce the skills in each content area.
5. Make a check-off list itemizing each skill in each content area, so you can check off areas as they are covered.
6. Make a chart of the resources and textbook chapters which cover each skill area.

C. REVIEW THE RECORDS

Examine previous records of children with an open mind. They can be useful in providing clues to identify children's needs and interests, but should not be used to prejudge children or their capabilities.

1. Make your parent phone calls before you review the records, so you have a personal image of the child before you acquire an on-paper one.
2. Review test scores, grades, reading and math levels and comments from previous teachers.
3. Take notes about strengths and weaknesses, adding them to the notes from the phone calls.
4. Recognize that the impressions you are developing can be changed at any time and that children are constantly growing and changing.
5. Emphasize positive qualities and try to get a sense of children's interests and ways to reach them.

D. SET UP THE CLASSROOM

It is important to create an environment conducive to working together for growth. The classroom sets up the opportunity for listening to children and letting them be responsible for their own learning.

1. Make a trial run to study the classroom.
2. Enter the classroom when you are relaxed and excited about the coming year.
3. If you had the same classroom last year, look around and draw a diagram of how the room had been arranged.
4. Note how the areas were used effectively. Reflect upon areas used most often—what worked and what didn't.
5. Look at the furniture you have, and consider ways it can be used.
6. Reflect upon your phone calls and review of the records to identify the interests of your new students.
7. Try to tie the children's interests to areas of the curriculum: math, science, social studies, reading, writing.
8. Leave for the first time with a rough sketch of how you might arrange the room.
9. Begin your own research to find items from everyday experience which relate to the children's interests.
10. Call parents and children and tell them when you will be setting up the room. Invite them to join in.
11. Bring in the items you have collected, and ask them to bring their contributions.
12. Leave the room purposely incomplete. Don't fill all of the bulletin boards, shelves, tables, etc. The children who haven't helped will want to bring things in later, and other interests will develop as the year progresses.
13. Brainstorm with the children as you work to set up the room. Include their ideas.

II. WITHIN THE FIRST WEEK OF SCHOOL

A. DEVELOP TRUST AND FOSTER CHOICE

The children have to understand, from the moment that they walk in the door, that this is a different classroom experience, one in which they will determine the course of their education.

1. Greet the children warmly, by name if possible, as they walk in the door.
2. Invite them to look around the room.
3. Ask them to identify the things in the classroom which they brought in or which relate to their interests.
4. Tell them they may choose a place to sit.
5. Prepare them for the first clearing meeting.
6. Include at least one textbook or workbook exercise on the first day, so that they can work in a way that is familiar to them.

B. CONDUCT THE FIRST CLEARING MEETING

More than a show-and-tell, the clearing meeting is an opportunity to be heard about whatever is on one's mind, so that each student can be present in the classroom to get work done.

1. Identify with the children an area in the room where the class will meet every day for the clearing meeting.
2. Share first in an open and honest way what you are like and what you hope to accomplish in the classroom.
3. Invite the children to share in the same way.
4. Demonstrate for the children complete acceptance of what they say. The group doesn't necessarily have to adopt an idea to acknowledge it. There is no insignificant contribution. Everyone matters.
5. Plan the first day with the students.
6. Have them list the activities they want to be involved in during the coming days. Your ideas count too.
7. Agree on an order with them.
8. Once you agree on a plan for the day, stick to it unless the group decides to alter it.

9. Acknowledge each child for sharing. Acknowledgment is different from praise.
10. Continue the clearing meeting at the beginning of the day throughout the year.
11. Use the clearing meeting to plan the day and to discuss any problems that arise.

C. RECORD CHILDREN'S REACTIONS TO FIRST DAY
Observing and recording anecdotally the children's responses to their first day adds one more dimension to the teacher's understanding of the students and their interests.
1. Write down at least a few descriptive words about each child.
2. Record anecdotally rather than judgmentally; e.g., "asked about bird's nest," rather than "likes birds"; "moved rapidly around room," rather than "hyperactive."
3. Pay particular attention to what seems to attract the children—what they seem interested in and what their learning style might be. How do they work—alone, in a group, silently, verbally, visually, numerically?
4. Add your comments to your record of the summer phone calls and your notes from previous records.

D. CONDUCT THE FIRST PARENT/CHILD/TEACHER PARTNERSHIP MEETING
A partnership produces a result. It is formed to accomplish a goal, not simply to exist. The goal in this case is the education of the children, and the vehicle is mutual trust, enthusiasm and respect.
1. Identify your thoughts about the year ahead before the meeting. Write them down.
2. Be excited about this opportunity for partnership.
3. Plan the meeting for early in the evening, so the children can participate.
4. Outline the time frame.

5. List some of the questions you might ask of parents; elicit their goals for their children.

6. Set up chairs in a way that works for you—either in traditional classroom style or in a circle.

7. Have name tags and a sign-in sheet ready.

8. Allow ten or fifteen minutes for coffee and mixing, and then begin the meeting.

9. Begin by sharing your commitment and telling them the purpose of the meeting.

10. Make it clear that what is said during the evening could have an impact on their children's education for the future.

11. Observe reactions of parents and children, to each other, to the teacher, to the group.

12. Ask members of the group to identify themselves and state why they came and what they hope to have happen. You might want to ask parents to describe a fun experience they had in school. You might want to ask children to mention one favorite interest.

13. Respect everyone's right to pass or refuse to participate.

14. Acknowledge each effort to contribute to the evening.

15. List some of the hopes for the evening on the blackboard.

16. Have fun yourself. Listen for the humor in what people say.

17. When everyone who wishes to has spoken, change the focus.

18. Ask everyone to take a partner, mixing parents and children wherever possible.

19. Request that one person in each partnership speak for two minutes on what he or she has heard so far. Then reverse the process. Specify that even if a partner stops speaking before the two minutes are up, he should be listened to in attentive silence.

20. Take a break—coffee, soda, mixing.

21. During the break, ask parents to talk about the question, "What is effective listening?" Children can mingle in a different area of the room and continue to talk with each other about interests they might have in common.

22. After the break, invite parents to share their observations about listening.

23. Describe your teaching style and the ways effective listening contributes to that style.

24. Ask the children to report on some of their interests and the connections they might have discovered in their conversations during the break.

25. Reflect your own excitement about these interests, and describe how they will lead to learning in the classroom.

26. Ask parents to be specific about their concerns, e.g. homework, testing, study habits, curriculum. List these on the board.

27. As a group, choose an issue to discuss at the next meeting. Have some possible topics ready in case there are few ideas.

28. Invite parents to call you with any concerns.

29. Set a date for the next meeting.

30. Continue to conduct parent/child/teacher partnership meetings every four to six weeks throughout the year.

E. BEGIN THE PROBLEM-SOLVING PROCESS

The children will learn to identify the problem, come up with alternative solutions and choose one.

1. Use the clearing meeting to solve group problems or dilemmas.

2. Begin with the most basic of problems, those they might encounter in the first few days, such as choosing cubbies, seats, working in different corners of the room.

3. Move to asking them what they like to do best, e.g., writing, drawing, counting, exploring the room.

4. Ask them to settle on an order of work for the day, either individually or as a group.

5. Accept and include all ideas.

6. When they do paper/pencil work, let them do it the way they are used to, so that their own questions arise, such as "Did I do this right?" or "Should I print or write?"

7. Respond to questions in a way that allows them to make decisions, e.g., What is your goal? Can you explain your work to me?

8. There are no wrong answers, just different ways of doing things. Help them to choose the ways that work best for them or the group.

F. DEVELOP THE FIRST INTEREST CHART

The purpose of the interest chart, initially, is to show the children that each of them has an interest, no matter how seemingly insignificant.

1. Use the clearing meeting time to begin the interest chart.
2. Have a chalk board or chart paper to record the interests.
3. Begin by saying, "Tell me what you are interested in and I will write it on the board." They have already spoken of interests when setting up the room and at the parent/child/teacher meeting.
4. As you write down their interests, ask them to categorize them, e.g., if they mention camels, lead them to the animal category.
5. Begin to make some simple connections between interests with lines drawn on the chart, e.g., camels and a desert, trains and tunnels.
6. Ask them what they might want to know about their interest.
7. Accept all responses.
8. Acknowledge all children for contributing.
9. Include the first interest chart with the first newsletter.

G. SEND HOME THE FIRST NEWSLETTER

The newsletter, which includes the first interest chart, validates for the children that something will happen as a result of their interests. They are sharing their interests with their parents and bringing their parents into the learning process.

1. Meet in a discussion circle.
2. Tell the children you are writing a newsletter which will include their interests.
3. Ask them to comment on what they hope to find out.
4. Include a comment or question from each child, in his or her own words.
5. Include your reflections as well.
6. Invite parents to participate in the finding out process. Ask them if they know anything about the children's interests they might like to share, by sending in materials or speaking to the class.
7. Tell them you will keep them posted as new interests and connections are developed.
8. Send newsletters weekly throughout the year, and include children's comments, reactions to visitors, subsequent interest charts, areas of the curriculum to be covered and invitations to parents.

H. INTRODUCE THE CURRICULUM

It is important for the children and their parents to know that you will help them connect their interests to the curriculum and that the curriculum will be covered by every child.

1. Write down sample interests on the board or on chart paper.
2. Connect each interest to the major curriculum areas, e.g., camels: science (biological description of camels), social studies (What cultures use camels as transportation?), reading (stories about camels, mythical and real), mathematics (population of camels).
3. Invite children to connect their own interests to these areas, in a general rather than specific way at first.
4. Do some formal and informal testing, and use texts and workbooks as needed to develop skills. Ask students how they might use the skill they have mastered, how it fits with their interest.

I. WORK OUT A PRELIMINARY TIME MANAGEMENT PLAN
1. Distribute a simple chart to each child every day.
2. Under "What I accomplished today," ask students to list the activities they worked on.
3. Under "What I learned today," ask them to identify the skills that were reinforced through each activity.
4. If it becomes apparent that the desired skill was not mastered, suggest other ways to work on the skill.
5. Under "What I'm working on," ask students to mention the unmastered skill or the incomplete project, and set a date for completion.
6. Use the students' basic time management plans to prepare your individual lesson plans for the following week. Connect the skills in the curriculum to their interests to create activities.
7. Encourage the students to use their plans to keep track of the skills they have mastered.
8. Prepare them to create a more complicated time management system later in the year.

J. DISTRIBUTE INDIVIDUAL RECORD BOOKS
More than a diary or journal, the record book provides an opportunity to jot down individual thoughts, drawings, scribbles, plans, anything that doesn't fit into the rest of the school day.
1. Make sure each child has a brand new notebook.
2. Make it clear that the notebook is each child's personal property, and that the rest of the class will value and respect his or her right to share the notebook or keep it private.
3. Provide enough time every day for working in record books.
4. Provide time every few days for sharing of record books—poems, drawings, thoughts, etc.
5. Respond to sharing with enthusiasm.
6. Try to connect work in record books with interests.

K. READ ALOUD

The children enjoy sharing good literature with their classmates without regard for differences in reading ability. Your reading aloud to them provides that opportunity.

1. Read aloud to the children every day.
2. Include literature that relates to the children's interests.
3. Ask for contributions and suggestions from the class.
4. Include books that would be too difficult for children to read on their own.

III. WITHIN THE FIRST FEW WEEKS OF SCHOOL

A. BEGIN THE RESEARCH PROCESS

The research process begins as soon as the first interest chart has been developed. The purpose is to develop the interests and look for patterns.

1. Review parent occupations and notes from parent phone calls.
2. Make a file of parent interests and careers to use as a resource.
3. Go to the library to locate and select books, both fiction and non-fiction, related to the first interest chart.
4. Check your resources and files from former years, to find related pictures and materials. Bring them to the classroom.
5. Check the newspaper every day for related information.
6. Make a list of agencies involved in the topic, visitors, places to visit.
7. Agree on a first visitor or trip.

B. ENTERTAIN A VISITOR

1. Decide on a visitor who will elaborate on one interest in the interest chart.
2. Have the children write letters inviting the visitor to speak.

3. Ask them to include questions that they personally would like to have answered.

4. When the visitor comes, allow plenty to time for questions and discussion.

5. Ask the visitor to suggest possible field trips related to the topic and possible related topics.

6. Have the children write thank you notes commenting on what they learned or would like to know more about.

C. DEVELOP THE BRAINSTORMING PROCESS

Brainstorming is used to make connections between interests and to focus on one particular interest area. Eventually, this process leads to a central theme that incorporates all of the children's interests.

1. Begin the brainstorming process after the first visitor has come to class.

2. Choose a focus word from the interest chart or from the first visitor's topic, e.g., "roads."

3. Use the same process you used to develop the interest chart.

4. Ask the children what they are interested in related to the focus word, "road"; e.g., bridges.

5. Accept all responses, even if the connections seem loose.

6. Use the new word or words to develop the interest further.

7. Invite a visitor to discuss a particular bridge, or take a class trip to see a bridge being built. The trip or visitor will invite further brainstorming, with a new focus word.

8. Produce a new interest chart from each brainstorming session. Each interest chart should make connections which lead you closer to choosing a theme.

9. Keep an open mind about what the theme will eventually be. Keep reinforcing interests of class members that may be unrelated to the new focus word. The class may decide to shift the focus or decide that the unrelated interest is in some way related after all.

10. Begin to create team projects related to the focus words.

D. SET UP TEAM PROJECTS

When children work with their peers toward a common goal, they cooperate out of a shared purpose and commitment. When they design the structure of their own learning, the learning is all the more significant.

1. Allow children whose interests are connected to develop a group project.
2. Make sure the project is related to the stated interests.
3. Be specific. Ask the children to define the project.
4. Have them make lists of what needs to be done—supplies, letters to write, people to contact.
5. Have them make a commitment as to time lines, dates for beginning and completion of project.
6. Make sure all members of the team are involved.
7. Develop their project worksheet with them.
8. Connect the project to the curriculum. Assign tasks for learning specific skills, and see that they incorporate that learning into the project.

E. BLEND IN THE CURRICULUM

Teaching the skills coincidental with children's interest or need to find out requires meticulous record-keeping. Parents and students need to know that one way or another every child will be exposed to every required skill during the year and will receive enough practice to master it.

1. Keep a curriculum guide (Scope and Sequence) handy.
2. Make a chart each week of the key areas you are working on.
3. Use the curriculum guide to check off the skills covered.
4. Note in a few words each week who has and who has not mastered the skills.
5. As you plan for each child or group in connection with the interest, create assignments from texts, workbooks and independent research that will address the skill.
6. Use those who have mastered the skill as resources for others.
7. When a particular group learns a skill, call the class together

in a discussion group with a blackboard handy, and have them share what they learned.

8. Make sure they tie the skill to their interest or the interest project they are working on.

9. Use assignments from text to reinforce the skill for the whole class, or ask students to research how another author has handled the same skill.

10. Ask guest experts to fill in the gaps. Tell the visitor what the students need to master, as well as what interests them.

11. Insist that the children are able to identify the skill they are working on: that they are able to speak the term, describe it and use it in connection with their interests.

12. Test judiciously, in small or whole group situations. Use results positively, to identify areas to work on.

13. Ask students to keep track of their own mastery through their time management plans. The plan book, the curriculum check list and the time management plans are a triple check to assure that all areas are covered with all children.

F. CONSTRUCT A TIME MANAGEMENT SYSTEM
Accurate time management plans act as part of a triple check, with the plan book and the curriculum check list, to assure that all areas of the curriculum are covered. They also serve to make the children aware of what they have accomplished, how to meet their commitments and how their skills mastery ties in with their interests.

1. Explain that the preliminary time management plans the students have been working from can prepare them for something more complicated.

2. Distribute second time management chart.

3. Describe each column of the chart and each possibility for connection to interests. Have children brainstorm about what might fit in each column.

4. Ask them to work out a sample day on the new plan, using a preliminary plan from the previous day or week. They

might work in small groups and create one single plan for a group.

5. Have them continue with individual plans.
6. At the end of each week, collect plans to aid in program planning for the next week.
7. Return plans to students so they can keep their own records of progress.

G. INTRODUCE THE THINKING SKILLS

It has become increasingly important, in our society, that children learn how to think at the same time as they are mastering skills. Some skills may become outdated. Thinking never will. Teaching according to interests is a perfect way to develop thinking skills.

1. Set up a bulletin board using the thinking words—observe, predict, assume, compare, summarize, conclude, etc.
2. Have children illustrate or define in their own words the thinking skills, e.g., guess for assume.
3. Use the words consciously and often, in everyday conversation. *Predict* what the new kid will look like. *Assume* that most students will be hungry at lunchtime. *Observe* that one child has on a new dress. *Hypothesize* that another stayed home because he wasn't feeling well. *Compare* the length of pencils, the color of crayons, the size of boxes, the number of papers.
4. Move to encouraging the children to use the words on trips, in reports and in class discussion. Make guesses, predictions or assumptions about where an animal lives, how people in another time prepared their meals, etc.
5. Correlate the thinking terms with what you are doing in the curriculum areas. Compare the characters in a story; hypothesize about mathematical problem solving; observe texture, color, odor in a science experiment; draw conclusions about what people in other cultures do for a living by the tools they use.

H. CONDUCT A SECOND PARENT/CHILD/TEACHER MEETING

The second meeting, conducted within a month of the first, reinforces the idea of a developing partnership and brings the curriculum into focus. It demonstrates, with the help of an invited resource person, how the curriculum and interests can be tied together.

1. Tell the group what happened in the classroom as a result of the last meeting.
2. Let the parents and children tell you what they hope to learn from the evening.
3. Ask the children to share one or two of the interest areas that have emerged in the classroom as predominant.
4. Introduce guest, who is an expert in one particular curriculum area.
5. Ask the guest to comment on the interests just described by the students, connecting his subject area to the interests. Highlight, in particular, those skills that must be acquired during the school year, and demonstrate how the skills can be mastered through activities connected with the interests.
6. After the break, invite other students to share something special they've been working on: stories, illustrations, numerical problems.
7. Invite parents to come up with connections to curriculum areas and suggest possible activities.
8. Plan together the next meeting, and ask for support for the projects developing in the classroom.

IV. AS THE YEAR CONTINUES

A. IDENTIFY THE THEME

Within the first two months, the interests of class members should come together to produce a single unifying theme, around which the learning for the year revolves. The theme inspires excitement, team spirit and a sense of accomplishment.

1. Conduct frequent brainstorming sessions to create new focus words and thus new interest charts.
2. During brainstorming sessions, make connections between interests or parts of interests by examining how focus words serve more than one interest; e.g., "bridge" may go with a road interest or a travel interest; "travel" may go with outer space or touring; "outer space" can connect with science fiction or astronauts. The connections are endless.
3. As the brainstorming and resultant interest charts take the class in new directions, watch for emerging patterns.
4. Head toward a theme with the greatest number of obvious connections to people's interests.
5. When most of the students feel connected to a possible theme, help the others tie in some aspect of their interests.
6. Repeat the brainstorming process, using the theme as a focus word, until all connections are made.
7. Identify the theme. Say it aloud and work with it until it becomes a whole class commitment.

B. DEVELOP AND EXPAND PROJECTS

Projects arise out of the theme development and in turn lead to the development of a unifying project, which leads to the necessity for creating more projects. The projects are a productive and satisfying way to acquire knowledge. Because they are tangible, they also demonstrate to others the knowledge acquired.

1. As small groups or teams report on already begun projects, brainstorm and make connections between the projects and the newly identified theme if possible. Some projects may have to be completed without a connection.
2. Other groups or teams will form to work on projects related to their interests within the theme; e.g., theme: city; project related to specific interest: build a tunnel.
3. Create a whole class project that incorporates the team projects; e.g., whole class project: build a model city; sam-

ple team projects: work on stores, costumes, tunnels, bridges.

4. Formulate other teams as needed to complete all class project. Everyone is involved.

5. Ask for assistance with overall project from parents, community members.

6. Invite outsiders—rest of school, parents, etc.—to see results of project; e.g., an original play, a major construction.

7. Continue to weave the curriculum and the thinking skills into the project.

C. CONTINUE REGULAR ACTIVITIES, INCREASING THE COMPLEXITY

1. Send weekly newsletters to keep alive the parent/child/teacher partnership. Include problems and their solutions, interest chart development, summaries of trips, projects, and visitors, comments from students, integration of the curriculum and future plans. Involve students in the writing. Always invite parents to participate.

2. Begin each day with the clearing meeting. Use the children's ideas for planning the day and solving problems in the classroom.

3. Allow time each day for the children to work in their record books. Provide opportunities for sharing items in the record book.

4. Conduct frequent brainstorming sessions to rework and refine the interest chart, thereby connecting areas of interest and including related curriculum areas.

5. Once the theme is identified, usually four to six weeks into the year, brainstorm frequently to make curriculum connections with the theme.

6. Read aloud to the children every day. Include literature that relates to the interests or to the theme.

7. Produce team projects related to interests within the theme, and produce an overall class project.

8. Complete a learning plan for each child every week, relating interests, theme or project to skills to be mastered.

9. Use the thinking skills consciously in every aspect of classroom interaction. The skills should become second nature and a product of creativity as much as logic.

10. Let every child experience being a coach/leader regularly, in the project team and in the class as a whole.

11. Be a partner in research, enthusiasm and creativity with every project team. Come up with ideas, respond to their ideas.

12. Create a network of support in the classroom. Use the clearing meeting or brainstorming session to elicit one team's support for another. It is possible for students to be interested in and contribute to the projects of others while still being true to their primary interest.

13. Become actively involved as a class in a real life problem, and do whatever is necessary—write letters, visit problem sites, make phone calls—to make a difference in the outcome.

14. Conduct parent/child/teacher partnership meetings every four to six weeks, and elicit parent support and involvement whenever possible.

V. AS THE YEAR CLOSES

A. COMPLETE THE WHOLE CLASS PROJECT

The whole class project is the culmination of the year's learning and thinking. Each member of the class will have made a slightly different contribution, and yet the result will be a team effort.

1. Plan that all team projects will come together in a major event, display or presentation sometime in May; e.g., all chapters of an original book will be typed and pasted together; a play will be presented with sets designed, actors

prepared and costumes made; an environment, such as an Indian village or an Egyptian pyramid, will be constructed with all of its parts.

2. Invite parents, school children, members of the community to the event or display.

3. Write thank you notes to all who helped, including parents, professional resources, workers.

4. Ask each project group to acknowledge and evaluate what other groups have accomplished toward the success of the overall project.

B. BRING CLOSURE TO THE YEAR

It is important for the children to feel a sense of completion and accomplishment, that there has been some conclusion to their activities.

1. Review the year by brainstorming with the children regarding what they learned, what they are good at, how they work with others, how they have grown.

2. Ask them to write in their time management plans what they still hope to accomplish.

3. Allow time to work in the record books, so they may reflect upon their view of themselves as they are now, compared to the beginning of the year.

4. Tie up any loose ends in the curriculum, citing in your weekly planning the areas still to be covered for individuals and the class.

5. Complete end of the year testing and evaluation.

6. Chart the children's progress in the curriculum areas, as information for the next year's teacher.

C. LOOK AHEAD

Lifetime learning suggests that what the children have learned will be useful to them all their lives. The self-confidence they have acquired and the methods of investigation they have practiced will serve them forever.

1. Make assumptions about what school will be like next year.
2. Ask children to list ways in which they can use what they learned this year, even with a different teacher, different subject matter and different classmates.
3. Discuss what didn't work in the classroom and how they might do things differently.
4. Brainstorm ways in which they can keep their interests alive.
5. Talk about real world problems and issues which will be of concern to them when they are older.
6. Plan a reunion for sometime during the summer.

Charts for Record-keeping

Pre-Work for Time Management

Name: _____ Date: _____

What I did today: _____

_____

_____

_____

_____

_____

What I learned today: _____

_____

_____

_____

_____

_____

What I'm still working on: _____

_____

_____

_____

_____

_____

_____

Name: _____ Date: _____ Day of the Week: _____

SUBJECT	TIME START	CONNECT SUBJECT WITH MY INTEREST	BOOKS & PAGE #s MATERIALS USED	WHAT I HAVE ACCOMPLISHED	TIME STOP
	:				:
	:				:
	:				:

Name: _____   Date: _____   Day of the Week: _____

SUBJECT	TIME START	CONNECT SUBJECT WITH MY INTEREST	BOOKS & PAGE #s MATERIALS USED	WHAT I HAVE ACCOMPLISHED	TIME STOP
MATH	:				:
READING	:				:
SCIENCE	:				:
SOCIAL STUDIES	:				:
LANGUAGE ARTS	:				:
HEALTH	:				:
PROJECTS	:				:

Team Project Worksheet

Project Title: _____

Team Leader: _____

Team Members: _____   _____

_____   _____

Describe Your Project: _____

_____

_____

_____

The Results You Want: _____

_____

_____

_____

Actions: By Whom: By When:

_____   _____   _____

_____   _____   _____

_____   _____   _____

_____   _____   _____

Resources and Supplies Needed: _____

_____

_____

Next Meeting Date: _____   Time: _____

Unfolding Self-Esteem

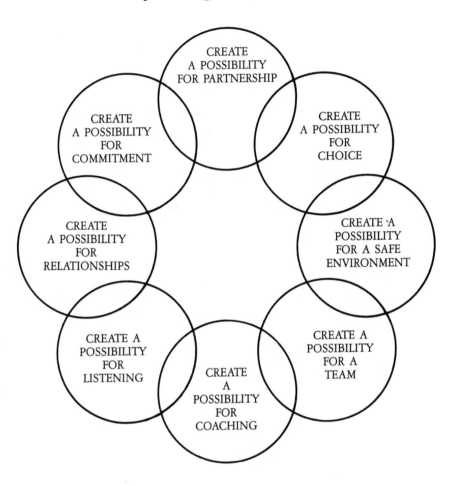

CREATE
A POSSIBILITY
FOR PARTNERSHIP

CREATE
A POSSIBILITY
FOR
COMMITMENT

CREATE
A POSSIBILITY
FOR
CHOICE

CREATE
A POSSIBILITY
FOR
RELATIONSHIPS

CREATE ·A
POSSIBILITY
FOR A SAFE
ENVIRONMENT

CREATE A
POSSIBILITY
FOR
LISTENING

CREATE
A
POSSIBILITY
FOR
COACHING

CREATE A
POSSIBILITY
FOR A
TEAM

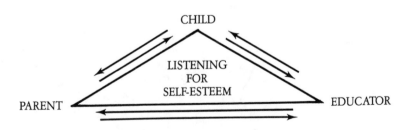

CHILD

LISTENING
FOR
SELF-ESTEEM

PARENT

EDUCATOR

Coaching

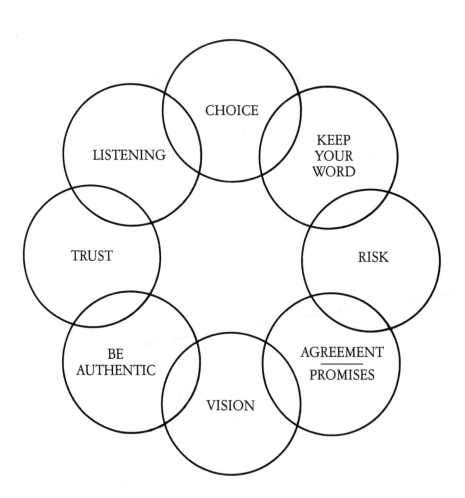

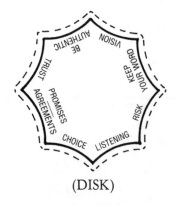

(DISK)

1. CUT DISK ALONG DOTTED LINE.
2. PLACE DISK IN CENTER OF COACHING RING.
3. ROTATE TO MAKE NEW CONNECTIONS.

Elaine Young has been a classroom teacher in New York for 28 years and lives in Purchase with her husband and two sons. Her students have covered the educational spectrum from kindergarten through graduate school. She is the producer and moderator of the Westchester Classroom, a weekly radio program. She has been guest lecturer and discussion leader at seminars and workshops for colleagues and has taught reading and language arts at New Paltz, Manhattanville and Marymount College. Mrs. Young is a course leader and community leader for the Education Network. She is the recipient of the Rotary Club of Hartsdale Service Above Self Award for 1980. Whether she is teaching children or adults, moderating a radio show or speaking to a group of concerned citizens, Mrs. Young retains the conviction that the best way to teach is to listen.

※

Robert Frelow has been the superintendent of schools in Greenburgh School District Number Seven, Hartsdale, New York, since 1974, having previously served as assistant superintendent of instruction in the same district. He received his Ph.D. from the University of California in 1970. Dr. Frelow has published numerous articles related to school policy and administration. This is his first collaboration on a book about an educational practice which he feels needs more administrative support. In his words, "Each life is *a blade of grass,* worthy of our love and attention."

※

Anne Kipp is a high school guidance counselor in Connecticut. She is the author of several articles and publications on counseling and education and the editor of two full-length manuscripts by educators. She has brought a counseling perspective to her work with Elaine Young, considering it paramount to preserve those words which convey the genuine love and respect for children so obvious in firsthand observation of Mrs. Young's classroom.

※

Barbara Dana has starred on and off Broadway and on TV, written novels and screenplays, recorded her own music and raised three sons. Three of her books are for children. For *Zucchini,* a book about a black-footed ferret, she received several awards, including the first Washington Irving Children's Book Choice Award, given annually to a Westchester County, New York, author. Her young adult novel, *Necessary Parties,* is a television film for PBS. Her commitments to children and to family have inspired her interest in Mrs. Young's teaching.

NEW

Openmind/Wholemind
Parenting & Teaching Tomorrow's Children Today

A book of powerful possibilities that honors the capacities, capabilities, and potentials of adult and child alike. Uses Modalities, Intelligences, Styles and Creativity to explore how the brain-mind system acquires, processes and expresses experience. Foreword by M. McClaren & C. Charles.
0-915190-45-1 $14.95
7 × 9   paperback
81 B/W photos 29 illus.

Present Yourself! *Captivate Your Audience With Great Presentation Skills*

Become a presenter who is a dynamic part of the message. Learn about Transforming Fear, Knowing Your Audience, Setting The Stage, Making Them Remember and much more. Essential reading for anyone interested in the art of communication. Destined to become the standard work in its field.
0-915190-51-6 paper $9.95
0-915190-50-8 cloth $18.95
6 × 9 paper/cloth. illus.

NEW

Unicorns Are Real
A Right-Brained Approach to Learning

Over 100,000 sold. The long-awaited "right hemispheric" teaching strategies developed by popular educational specialist Barbara Vitale are now available. Hemispheric dominance screening instrument included.
0-915190-35-4 $10.95
8½ × 11 paperback, illus.

Unicorns Are Real Poster

Beautifully-illustrated. Guaranteed to capture the fancy of young and old alike. Perfect gift for unicorn lovers, right-brained thinkers and all those who know how to dream.
For classroom, office or home display.

JP9027 $4.95
19 × 27 full color

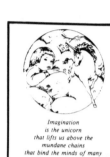

*Imagination
is the unicorn
that lifts us above the
mundane chains
that bind the minds of many
and flies us on fantastic wings
to a place where dreams DO come true.*

Practical Application, Right Hemisphere Learning Methods

Audio from Barbara Vitale. Discover many practical ways to successfully teach right-brained students using whole-to-part learning, visualization activities, color stimuli, motor skill techniques and more.
JP9110 $12.95
Audio Cassette

Don't Push Me, I'm Learning as Fast as I Can

Barbara Vitale presents some remarkable insights on the physical growth stages of children and how these stages affect a child's ability, not only to learn, but to function in the classroom.

JP9112 $12.95
Audio Cassette

Tapping Our Untapped Potential

This Barbara Vitale tape gives new insights on how you process information. Will help you develop strategies for improving memory, fighting stress and organizing your personal and professional activities.

JP9111 $12.95
Audio Cassette

Free Flight *Celebrating Your Right Brain*

Journey with Barbara Vitale, from her uncertain childhood perceptions of being "different" to the acceptance and adult celebration of that difference. A book for right-brained people in a left-brained world. Foreword by Bob Samples.
0-915190-44-3 $8.95
5½ × 8½ paperback, illus.

"He Hit Me Back First"
Self-Esteem through Self-Discipline

Simple techniques for guiding children toward self-correcting behavior as they become aware of choice and their own inner authority.
0-915190-36-2 $10.95
8½ × 11 paperback, illus.

Learning To Live, Learning To Love

An inspirational message about the importance of love in everything we do. Beautifully told through words and pictures. Ageless and timeless.

0-915190-38-9 $7.95
6 × 9 paperback, illus.

Pajamas Don't Matter:
(or What Your Baby Really Needs)

Here's help for new parents everywhere! Provides valuable information and needed reassurances to new parents as they struggle through the frantic, but rewarding, first years of their child's life.
0-915190-21-4 $5.95
8½ × 11 paperback, full color

From Two To Three Years:
Social Competence

Shows important ways children define their identity by learning to play with other children, exploring the world, mastering the art of communication, and developing their senses of imagination and humor.

0-935266-03-8 $5.95
8½ × 11 paper, B/W photos

Feelings Alphabet

Brand-new kind of alphabet book full of photos and word graphics that will delight readers of all ages.''. . .lively, candid. . .the 26 words of this pleasant book express experiences common to all children.'' *Library Journal*
0-935266-15-1 $7.95
6 × 9 paperback, B/W photos

The Parent Book

A functional and sensitive guide for parents who want to enjoy every minute of their child's growing years. Shows how to live with children in ways that encourage healthy emotional development. Ages 3-14.

0-915190-15-X $9.95
8½ × 11 paperback, illus.

Aliens In My Nest
SQUIB Meets The Teen Creature

Squib comes home from summer camp to find that his older brother, Andrew, has turned into a snarly, surly, defiant, and non-communicative adolescent. *Aliens* explores the effect of Andrew's new behavior on Squib and the entire family unit.
0-915190-49-4 $7.95
8½ × 11 paperback, illus.

NEW

Hugs & Shrugs
The Continuing Saga of SQUIB

Squib feels incomplete. He has lost a piece of himself. He searches every where only to discover that his missing pieces has fallen in and not out. He becomes complete again once he discovers his own inner-peace.

0-915190-47-8 $7.95
8½ × 11 paperback, illus.

NEW

Moths & Mothers/ Feather & Fathers
A Story About a Tiny Owl Named SQUIB

Squib is a tiny owl who cannot fly. Neither can he understand his feelings. He must face the frustration, grief, fear, guilt and loneliness that we all must face at different times in our lives. Struggling with these feelings, he searches, at least, for understanding.

0-395-36555-4 $7.95
8½ × 11 paperback, illus.

Hoots & Toots & Hairy Brutes
The Continuing Adventures of SQUIB

Squib—who can only toot—sets out to learn how to give a mighty hoot. His attempts result in abject failure. Every reader who has struggled with life's limitations will recognize their own struggles and triumphs in the microcosm of Squib's forest world. A parable for all ages from 8 to 80.
0-395-39503-8 $7.95
8½ × 11 paperback, illus.

The Turbulent Teens
Understanding Helping Surviving

"This book should be read by every parent of a teenager in America. . .It gives a parent the information needed to understand teenagers and guide them wisely."—Dr. Fitzhugh Dodson, author of *How to Parent, How to Father,* and *How to Discipline with Love.*
0-913091-01-4 $8.95
6 × 9 paperback.

Whose Child Cries
Children of Gay Parents Talk About Their Lives

Straightforward and heartfelt explanations help make this book a valuable resource on homosexuality.

Foreword by Eda LeShan, columnist for Woman's Day Magazine.

0-915190-39-7 paperback $8.95
0-915190-40-0 cloth $16.95
5½ × 8½ paperback/cloth

TA For Tots
(and other prinzes)
Over 500,000 sold.

This innovative book has helped thousands of young children and their parents to better understand and relate to each other. Ages 4-9.
0-915190-12-5 $12.95
8½ × 11 paper, color, illus.

TA For Tots, Vol. II

Explores new ranges of feelings and suggests solutions to problems such as feeling hurt, sad, shy, greedy, or lonely.
Ages 4-9.
0-915190-25-7 $12.95
8½ × 11 paper, color, illus.

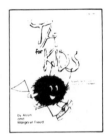

TA For Tots Coloring Book

Constructive, creative coloring fun! The charming *TA For Tots* characters help show kids that taking care of their feelings is OK! Ages 2-9.
0-915190-33-8 $1.95
8½ × 11 saddle stitched, illus.

TA Today I'm OK Poster

Cheerful, happy TA creatures help convey the most positive, upbeat message to be found. Perfect for brightening your room or office.
JP9002 $3.00
19 × 27 full color poster

TA for Kids
(and grown-ups too)
Over 250,000 sold.

The message of TA is presented in simple, clear terms so youngsters can apply it in their daily lives. Warm Fuzzies abound. Ages 9-13.
0-915190-09-5 $9.95
8½ × 11 paper, color, illus.

TA For Teens
(and other important people)
Over 100,000 sold.

Using the concepts of Transactional Analysis. Dr. Freed explains the ups and downs of adulthood without talking down to teens. Ages 13-18.
0-915190-03-6 $12.95
8½ × 11 paperback, illus.

Original Warm Fuzzy Tale
Learn about "Warm Fuzzies" firsthand.
Over 100,000 sold.

A classic fairytale...with adventure, fantasy, heroes, villains and a moral. Children (and adults, too) will enjoy this beautifully illustrated book.
0-915190-08-7 $7.95
6 × 9 paper, full color, illus.

Songs of The Warm Fuzzy
"All About Your Feelings"

The album includes such songs as Hitting is Harmful, Being Scared, When I'm Angry, Warm Fuzzy Song, Why Don't Parents Say What They Mean, and I'm Not Perfect (Nobody's Perfect).
JP9003R/C $12.95
LP Record Album/Cassette

Tot Pac *(Audio-Visual Kit)*

Includes 5 filmstrips, 5 cassettes, 2 record LP album. A *Warm Fuzzy I'm OK* poster, 8 coloring posters, 10 Warm Fuzzies. 1 *TA for Tots* and 92 page *Leader's Manual.* No prior TA training necessary to use Tot Pac in the classroom! Ages 2-9.
JP9032 $150.00
Multimedia program

Kid Pac *(Audio-Visual Kit)*

Teachers, counselors, and parents of pre-teens will value this easy to use program. Each *Kid Pac* contains 13 cassettes, 13 filmstrips, 1 *TA For Kids,* and a comprehensive *Teacher's Guide,* plus 10 Warm Fuzzies. Ages 9-13.
JP9033 $195.00
Multimedia Program